VOICE AND SELF

VOICE AND SELF

A Handbook of Personal Voice Development Therapy

Ingeburg Stengel
and
Theo Strauch

Translated by Arabella Spencer

'an association in which the free development of each
is the condition of the free development of all'

FREE ASSOCIATION BOOKS / LONDON / NEW YORK

First published in the United Kingdom 2000 by
FREE ASSOCIATION BOOKS
57 Warren Street, London W1P 5PA

Original edition published by Klett-Cotta, Stuttgart, Germany,
represented by the Cathy Miller Foreign Rights Agency, London.
© Klett-Cotta, J.G. Cotta'sche Buchhandlung Nachfolger GmbH,
gegr. 1659, Stuttgart 1996
© English language edition Free Association Books Ltd 2000
Translation © Arabella Spencer 2000

Originally published in German as:
Stimme und Person
Personale Stimmentwicklung. Personale Stimmtherapie.

The right of Ingeburg Stengel and Theo Strauch to be identified as the
authors of this work has been asserted by them in accordance with the
Copyright, Designs and Patents Act 1988.

A CIP catalogue record for this book is available from the British Library.

ISBN 1 85343 500 7

Designed and produced for the publisher by Chase Production Services
Printed in the European Union by Athenaeum Press, Gateshead, England

Contents

Preface   x

Part I   Concept

1. Voice and Self   3
   '*Personare*'   3
   Voice and Self as Instrument   4
   Voice and Self in Treatment   6

2. Person-Oriented Voice Therapy – PVT   8
   Basic Idea   8
   From Voice Function to the Self   8
   From Person to Voice Function   11
   The First Step into Person-oriented Voice Work   12
   Embarking on Self-reflection   13
   Understanding What the Voice Wants to Say   15
   Taking Charge and Responsibility for One's Own
   Treatment   17
   The Functional and Personal(ity) Levels of Voice Therapy
   Exercises   17
   Functional Level   18
   Personal Level   19
   Concentrated Work on the Body as a Basis of PVT   20
   Functional and Personal Meaning of Work on the Body   20
   Proprioception and Imagination   21
   Substance and Objectives of Work on the Body in PVT   22
   The Relationship Between Therapist and Client in PVT   25
   The Therapist as a Person   25
   The Therapist as Method   26
   The Relationship between Therapist and Client   26
   Consequences for Therapeutical Work on the Voice   27
   Transfer as a Consciously Executed, Permanent Process
   of Change   28
   The Problem of Transfer   28
   Transfer as a Process of Behavioural Change   29
   Voice Awareness as the Objective of Vocal Work   30

Part II   Anatomical and Physiological Aspects Seen from Functional and Personal Perspectives

3. Outline   36

4. Breathing   38
   Quiet Breathing   38
      Inspiration   38
      Expiration   39
      Abdomen-Flanks Breathing   39
      Rhythm of Breathing   40
   Speech Breathing   40
      Valve Function of Voice and Articulation   41
      Reflex Breath Completion   41
      Breath Rhythm Timed Phonation   42
      Inspiratory Countertension during Phonation (Support)   42

5. Voice Production (Phonation)   44
   A Tone is Formed from Air   44
      Closure of the Vocal Folds   44
      Vocal Fold Vibration   45
      Pitch   47
      Volume   48
      Interfering Factors   48
   Sound is Created from a Tone   49
      Resonance in the Vocal Tract   49
      Upper Partials   50
      Tonal Colour (Timbre)   51

6. Articulation   52
   Articulatory Organs   52
   Formation of Speech Sounds   52
   Articulation as a Means of Expression   53

7. Tonus and Intention   55
   Body Tension and Intention   55
   Body Tension and Posture   56

Part III   Exercises

8. Introduction to Exercises   59
   Sources of the Exercises   59

Division of the Collection of Exercises 60
Description of the Exercises 61
The Functional Level 61
The Personal Level 61

9. Collection of Exercises 63
Tonus
Regulation of tonus 65
Exercise 1: Lying down 65
Exercise 2: Comparing tonus 67
Exercise 3: Sitting 69
Exercise 4: Standing 71
Exercise 5: Massaging the feet 73
Work on the spinal column 75
Exercise 6: Shifting pressure using the ground 75
Exercise 7: Pressing into the ground 77
Physiological posture when sitting, standing and
walking 79
Exercise 8: Sitting 79
Exercise 9: Standing 81
Exercise 10: Walking 83
Work on the abdominal-pelvic region 85
Exercise 11: Sensitising the sacrum 85
Exercise 12: Rotating the pelvis 87
Exercise 13: Centring 89
Loosening of the musculature of the shoulders,
neck and throat 91
Exercise 14: Lying down 91
Exercise 15: Sitting 93
Exercise 16: Loosening up the shoulders 95
Loosening of the area of articulation and phonation 96
Exercise 17: With a stick 96
Exercise 18: With hands 98
Exercise 19: Sinus exercise 99
Exercise 20: Relaxing in the throat region 101
Breathing 103
Rhythm of breath and breathing areas 104
Exercise 21: Quiet breathing 104
Exercise 22: Expansion of breathing areas 106
Breath Rhythm Timed Phonation according to
Coblenzer and Muhar 108
Exercise 23: Perceiving reflex breath completion 108

Exercise 24: Practising relaxation   110
Exercise 25: With words and sentences   112
Exercise 26: Apportioning of texts   114
Inspiratory countertension (support)   116
Exercise 27: Consciousness of countertension   116
Exercise 28: Sounding into the pelvis   118
Phonation   121
   Producing Resonance Space in the Vocal Tract   122
   Exercise 29: Yawning exercise   122
   Exercise 30: Drinking exercise   123
   Physiological speaking voice register   125
   Exercise 31: Humming   125
   Exercise 32: Chewing exercise   127
   Perception of resonance throughout the whole body   129
   Exercise 33: Vowel spaces   129
   Exercise 34: Directional sounding of tones   131
   Resonance throughout the whole body while speaking   133
   Exercise 35: With syllables   133
   Exercise 36: With words   135
   Exercise 37: Series of words and sentences   137
   Position of sound, vowels and syllables   139
   Exercise 38: Consciousness of the position of sound   139
   Exercise 39: Use of vowels   141
   Exercise 40: Final syllables   143
   Work on the dynamics of the voice and the capacity
   to modulate   145
   Exercise 41: Increasing sound level   145
   Exercise 42: Modulation   147
   Exercise 43: Calling voice   149
Articulation   151
   Exercise 44: Formation of vowels   152
   Exercise 45: Being conscious of consonant formation   154
   Exercise 46: Speaking with a cork in your mouth   155
   Exercise 47: Forming of consonants   156

10. Suggestions for the Transfer   158
   Transfer Exercises   158
      Balance between Attention Directed Internally and
      Externally   158
      Increasing Level of Difficulty   159
   Aids and Options for Transfer   160

Part IV   Therapeutic Procedure in PVT

11. The Structure of Therapy — 165

12. Conducting the Exercises — 167
    Selecting an Exercise — 167
    Exercise Procedure — 169
        Motivation of Clients — 169
        The Subject of 'Demonstrating – Imitating' — 169
        Using Experimenting as a Method — 170
        'Homework' — 170
    Work on the Personal Level — 172
        Reflection — 172
        Reacting to Reflection — 174
        The Boundary between PVT and Psychotherapy — 174

13. Personal Aspects of Specific Disorders — 177
    Organic Voice Disorders — 177
        The Functional Side of Organic Voice Disorders — 177
        Personal and Organic Voice Disorders — 179
    Disorders of Children's Voices — 181
        Working with Children — 181
        Working with Parents — 182
    Disorders of the Singing Voice — 183
        The Singing Voice as a Special Function — 183
        Amateur Singers in Voice-therapeutic Treatment — 185
        Taking Care of the Voice — 186
        Of the Fortune and Misfortune of Professional Singers — 186
        Professional Singers in Voice Therapy — 187

14. Goals of PVT — 190
    What to Expect from Voice Therapy — 190
    Consequences for the Procedural Method — 191
    Understanding and Aims of Voice Therapy within PVT — 191

Bibliography — 193
Index — 197

Preface

Various professions are occupied with the voice, each with different objectives. Singing education is the oldest field and its objective is to train professional singers or to enable laymen to make proper use of their singing voice. Elocution is concerned with the speaking voice, predominantly of people who are in speaking professions, for example, actors or radio announcers.

Proceeding on the basis of medical diagnoses, voice therapy is concerned with organic or functional voice disorders and treats patients who have complaints or whose ability to communicate is impaired.

More recently a further field has come into being which we call 'voice development'. In the sense of personality development, it is concerned with developing individual vocal potential and vocal identity.

It is not easy to draw the boundaries between the various fields. The training of the singing or speaking voice for professional purposes ideally also involves personal development. Professional speakers or singers also often seek the help of speech or voice therapists because their voices have become impaired.

There is often only a minimal, gradual and very diversely perceived difference between a voice function that is considered as being normal and a voice disorder. This makes it particularly difficult to separate the fields of voice therapy and voice development from one another. In the course of our exposition we refer to both fields, and when we speak of therapy it should be understood that we are also talking about voice development. It is for this reason that we have adopted the extensive use of the term client instead of patient.

What these fields of work on the voice have in common is the training of the voice production function. Their objectives, however, are different.

Whilst singing education and elocution are concerned with achieving improved vocal performance for particular purposes, voice therapy and voice development are only concerned with the healthy voice or with achieving optimal vocal performance.

In order to achieve a particular kind of performance, a particular type of training is necessary. For example, ballet dancing is only learnt through lessons and intensive training. Walking, on the other hand, is not learnt through special training. Everyday language use is also learnt without specialised training, provided that all the necessary organs are intact.

The question arises as to why not everybody is able to develop their voice optimally or why, despite the apparent healthy state of the voice organ, the voice is sometimes no longer functional.

There seems to be something else that influences the voice. This something lies in the psycho-mental part of a person, and it can obstruct the functioning of an organ. This means that the unity of body, soul and spirit of a person always needs to be taken into consideration when working on the voice. This is of particular importance in the case of therapy for vocal disorders or in voice development since this is the point at which training the voice hits a barrier. What we are dealing with is more than just the training of a function. This book aims to shed light on what this 'more' entails.

The concept 'Person-Oriented Voice Development' ['*Personale Stimmtherapie*'] was developed by Ingeburg Stengel. It is the result of her many years of practical work with patients as a speech therapist, from work with groups of clients who work in speech-intensive professions (teachers, educators, managers) and, last but not least, from working with colleagues and looking at their experiences with their own voices.

During this work problems kept cropping up: despite intensive training of the vocal function, even if conducted over a longer period of time, the transfer of the practised into everyday language frequently presented problems. It seemed that practice alone was insufficient for achieving long-term vocal change. In addition, what became obvious was that even voice therapists were not always able to use their voices in the way 'they should be used'. Here the essential connection between voice and self became clear, as did the contradiction between theory and practice. It was possible to find a wealth of theoretical statements about the connection between voice and self in specialised literature, yet the prevailing approaches to voice therapy, being predominantly practice-oriented, did not seem to be taking this fact into account.

Ingeburg Stengel felt there was a need to develop a concept for 'person-oriented' work on the voice, that is, work that looked at the person as a whole rather than narrowly concentrating on the vocal function.

In his work with voice patients, Theo Strauch also experienced these contradictions, and went in search of what he felt was lacking in voice therapies.

In his search he came across Ingeburg Stengel. In her seminar 'Person-Oriented Voice Therapy' he found confirmation of his own ideas about how the voice should be worked upon, which, despite his having given them thought since the time of his own training, were not yet fully enough formed to allow him to take a definite stance.

Furthermore, in his capacity as a trainer of speech therapists he felt that there was an urgent need to define voice therapy procedures more clearly and to make them comprehensible for students.

Through the constant correspondence between both authors, based on the mutual understanding of voice disorders, the idea and need arose to aim person-oriented work on the voice at a wider audience. The concept was reworked and expanded upon, eventually taking the form in which it is presented in this book. It has been written for people belonging to the professions mentioned above who, in either an instructional or therapeutic role, are concerned with the voice and are interested in the personal aspect of the voice. It addresses people whose professional life depends on vocal performance. It also addresses patients who are in voice therapy and would like to learn more.

The book is divided into four main parts.

In Part I the connection between voice and self and the concept of Person-Oriented Voice Therapy (PVT), based on this connection, are described.

Part II describes the anatomical foundation and physiology of the voice in a manner comprehensible to the general reader. In doing so, it offers the interested layperson an understanding of the vocal function, as well as providing voice therapists with the basis for clearer explanations for their clients.

Part III contains an extensive collection of exercises that can serve both voice therapists and people practising on their own who wish to achieve improved vocal performance, as well as people who wish to continue voice therapy alone having initially seen a therapist.

Part IV is aimed primarily at voice therapists. It contains suggestions on therapeutic procedure and elucidates particular disorders of the voice with which speech therapy has to deal.

The book *Voice and Self* is based on professional practice and is intended for practical work on the voice. It is also addressed to everybody who is interested in the voice, who thinks about the phenomenon of voice and who considers the voice to be something fundamental to being human.

Ingeburg Stengel, Munich
Theo Strauch, Cologne   *August 1995*

Part I
Concept

1
Voice and Self

'Personare'

From the perspective of physiology, the voice can be understood as resulting from an interplay between various parts of our organism. Roughly distinguished, they are: breathing, which serves as the compression chamber; the larynx, in which tone is created; and the space above the larynx, which is described as the vocal tract and which is the place where sound is formed and in which speech sounds occur. The concrete combined working of these components is explained in detail in Part II.

The voice is, however, more than simply the result of these various processes.

The connection between voice and person was already well known in classical antiquity. Of Socrates it is said that, when meeting people for the first time, he called upon them to 'Speak so that I can see you'. He saw them by discerning the sound of their voices.

Gundermann (1994) describes the voice as the 'deep carrier' of language: 'But the voice is reserved for the wholly intimate. It is the "deep carrier" of language. The voice is capable of altering the meaning of a word, sentence or conversation through different subliminal tonal colourings, and indeed to do so substantially.'

It is interesting that the linguistic roots of the term 'person' are also associated with the voice.

The term is derived from the Latin 'persona' and originally referred to an actor's mask.

From 'persona' we get 'personare'. The concept 'personare' was described by Behrend in a radio broadcast on 28 November 1981 entitled 'The World is Sound':

The word for sounding through in Latin is 'personare'. The concept of the person, the idea of the person, what makes a person a person in the first place, an unmistakable unique personality is subject to a tonal imagination: personare – through sound.

Voice is therefore what is specific to a person, is what sounds, is audible. We can be recognised because of our voices even if we say only a single word over the telephone. Our voices reflect our personality and current mental state. We all constantly experience how often this is the case and how intimately our voice function is linked to ourselves as whole people. In a dispute it may, for example, be important to argue practically and to be fully in command, but in the process our voice may play a trick on us, indicating our emotional state and therefore sounding tearful or harsh. We have all had these or similar experiences with our voices, meaning that the close connection between voice and self can be experienced on a personal level.

Voice and Self as Instrument

It is widely believed that the voice is a controllable instrument. People seek to be able to play this instrument; one they expect always to function, irrespective of differences of situation.

It is astounding that the idea of a perfect voice exists even in circles of specialists, despite all that is known about the connection between voice and self. This idea leads to the expectation that voice therapists, as role models, should be 'in control' of their voices.

To a certain extent this is also possible through a learnt vocal technique. However, authenticity, that is, 'being in tune with oneself', gets lost and our behaviour becomes incongruent. In other words, what we say and how we say it is not consistent and the message that the partner in the conversation receives is unclear. If we want to be authentic we must accept that our voice does not always obey our wishes. It is not the voice that is the instrument but the whole person.

> There is a ... form of reaction that I have called 'congruent' or 'fluent'. With this form of reaction all parts of the message point in the same direction – the voice speaks words which correspond to facial expression, posture and tone of voice. (Satir, 1993: 95 [translated from the German])

The question that presents itself is that of how the misunderstanding came about that vocal behaviour can only be changed through the use of a specific technique without a person somehow being affected by it.

The causes presumably lie in the origin of the exercises offered for vocal improvement. They emanate predominantly from the field of vocal training, singing education or speech training.

The aim of this sort of work is to train the voice for aesthetic communication, that is, for speaking on stage or on the radio, or for singing. This mannered speech cannot be compared to the personal and spontaneous verbal expression of a speaker since the text exists in a concrete form and is merely interpreted by the speaker. It even makes a difference if a speaker presents self-formulated thoughts or whether he or she says something spontaneously. The speaker's vocal behaviour may differ considerably. To give an example:

A vicar's voice sounds much better during a sermon than it does when using colloquial language throughout the rest of the day. During the sermon he has a pre-formulated text in front of him, which he presents with the aim of communicating it to his listeners as well as he can. In so doing he assumes a different role, which already becomes apparent from his outward posture. He is standing erect and comfortably in the pulpit. In other situations, in conversation for example, he not only looks completely different but sounds different as well. Slumped in a chair, deliberately speaking softly, withdrawn, his voice suddenly sounds narrow, strangled or grating, and this causes him problems in the long run.

This example shows that even an existing 'good' vocal model is not always available, that is to say, it may be dependent on the situation or person. This phenomenon becomes a problem for voice therapists in their work. As a rule it is not difficult to learn a new kind of vocal behaviour as long as it is only applied in a practice situation. Its transfer into everyday language, on the other hand, often causes extreme difficulties (see Chapter 2). What is ignored is that the voice is the expression of the self, which means that a change in vocal behaviour is only possible on a long-term basis if something changes in the overall behaviour of the person. Something more needs to happen than the mere application of something newly learnt.

Wirth (1995: 187) writes in this connection: 'Almost all patients have a personal vocal image. For this reason patients often show a negative reaction towards the new voice. The patient must therefore see the necessity of developing and accepting a new voice.'

Voice and Self in Treatment

If we take the connection between voice and self seriously then this must have consequences for work on the voice, be it voice therapy or voice development.

For a long time voice therapy restricted itself solely to voice exercises and, occasionally, breathing exercises. It is only recently that the significance of body tonus for vocal production has been recognised and integrated into therapeutic practice. Furthermore, although it may not be universally confirmed, according to the general findings of psychosomatic medicine it is understood that the voice also belongs to the organs by means of which psychological problems express themselves, possibly leading to illness.

This has led to psychotherapy being used for the treatment of patients with vocal disorders. Psychotherapy is necessary in all cases where psychological problems are so predominant that work on the voice function is not yet possible or grinds to a halt.

But even in the cases where the need for psychotherapy is not apparent, the fact that voice and self are inseparable must be acknowledged. Voice therapy reduced to purely functional training quickly reaches a point at which no further treatment is possible. From all this we can conclude that:

> **Voice therapy is an independent field between functional training and psychotherapy.**

The following example serves to clarify this:

For reasons unknown to a successful 38-year-old opera singer, her vocal performance has deteriorated considerably. Due to the success she has experienced until now she rules out the possibility of faulty technique. During an examination by an ENT specialist an organic cause is not identified. The doctor prescribes speech therapy.

The singer is in despair because the audience reacts by booing her. Her fear of going on stage increases day by day, which leads to her voice's deteriorating further. She finds herself in a vicious circle. An investigation of her anamnesis reveals that the patient is going through a difficult life crisis. She is at an age where she increasingly fears that her desire to have a child will remain unfulfilled and that her career as a soprano is over. In discussing her anamnesis the patient for the first time makes the connection between her voice and her psychological situation.

Although the vocal disorder in this example clearly has psychological causes, it was the need for voice therapy and not psychotherapy that was indicated. In the first instance the patient needed quick help to get through the next few performances, but she also required assistance in her current situation of conflict. In conjunction with conversations the patient was stabilised through work on the body and breathing exercises, and her technique with regard to non-physiological processes was checked. At this time it remained open whether and to what extent the client wanted to work on underlying problems.

It was interesting that her first performance after the initial conversation went off smoothly and no negative reactions were shown by the audience.

Person-Oriented Voice Therapy attempts to define the area between functional training and psychotherapy and to make the unity of voice and self the basis of practical work.

2

Person-Oriented Voice Therapy – PVT

Basic Idea

The basic idea of Person-Oriented Voice Therapy (PVT) is:

> **From the voice function to the self (person) –**
> **from the self (person) to the voice function**

From Voice Function to the Self

In the previous chapter the link between voice and self was described. The conclusion drawn was that work on the voice, whether conscious or subconscious, is always also work on the self.
    This may be realised in different ways:

1. Neither therapist nor client really makes a conscious connection between voice and self. The symptom is, however, positively influenced through exercises and a new vocal behaviour can be learnt and effortlessly integrated into everyday language. In this way the client has widened his or her possibilities, as a person too, and has got rid of the problem. Unfortunately, this rarely happens.
2. Again the two people are not aware of the link between voice and self, that is, they 'overlook' it. The treatment grinds to a halt and it is not possible to achieve an improvement by means of functional training alone. Or: the symptom can be cured but the underlying problem is not recognised. The likelihood of a relapse or a shift of symptoms is very high in this instance.
3. Therapist and client go in search of the meaning of the symptom. The connection is recognised. The symptom improves and at the same time a conscious developmental step is taken.

4. The client has recognised the connection but cannot decide about working on a different mode of conduct. Either a part of what has been learnt can be converted and the client lives with fewer complaints, or the treatment is brought to an end. However, in both cases it is clear that vocal behaviour is not separable from overall behaviour.
5. The connection is sought but not found. The treatment grinds to a halt. Or: the problems underlying the voice disorder are revealed but in actual fact turn out to be quite serious. In both cases psychotherapy is indicated.

PVT proceeds on the basis of (3) and aims to drawn attention to the link between voice and self. The work then either results in a solution (3) or to a partial solution (4) or leads to psychotherapeutic treatment (5).

The starting point is work on the voice function with the aim of achieving optimal functionality. In voice functional training, work on the self is combined with the goal of making a change in voice function and may be experienced as a behavioural change. A central idea of PVT is thus:

**Work on the voice
is conscious work on the self.**

To accept vocal work as work on the whole self requires the willingness on the part of the client to get involved in this process. In other words, whether clients want to work on their self or not must remain their decision. What PVT seeks to clarify is that a change in voice is not separable from a change in overall behaviour. Moreover, work on a personal level should facilitate the transfer, the jumping of the 'hurdle'. By way of example:

A young man is seeking treatment for the following problem:

At work he finds that he is increasingly required to present his company's work to large groups of people. Because his voice is very quiet and monotonous he is constantly asked to speak up.

He tries to speak louder but the vocal technique he uses, namely that of exertion and muscle power, is not right and leads to his regularly being hoarse after presentations.

This induces him to speak almost in a whisper, in an attempt to spare his voice, which, from a physiological point of view, is actually just as strenuous.

Moreover, now the audience often has to ask him to speak up so that he can be understood. He finally becomes so unsure of himself that his voice fails him completely.

In therapy the patient very quickly comes to understand that he can only achieve a capable and resilient voice by means of resonance and not through exerting pressure. The initial humming exercises that reveal the sound of his voice are successful. As soon as his voice is directed outwards, in this case towards the therapist, the patient shies away, like a horse confronted with a hurdle that is too high.

His life history reveals what is probably keeping him from achieving a powerful voice. His father has a loud, melodious voice and would have liked to have become a singer. The son experiences his father as dominant and as relishing being the centre of attention. He clearly wants to differentiate himself from his father, who is a successful businessman. Unlike his father, he is interested in ecological problems and chose a job in this field. He is suspicious of the idea of being a 'tough and strong man' like his father. For him, other values are important. A big and loud voice has negative connotations for him. This is the reason why he constantly tries to suppress his own voice.

After he has understood what is going on underneath, he is able to approach work on his voice in a completely different way. He feels that his therapist understands his desire to be different from his father. Together they embark on the careful search for 'his' voice, a voice which, although it is powerful and melodious, is also soft and does not overpower the listener.

In this example the meaning of the symptom was recognised and the client was able to change his attitude and behaviour. His symptoms, his quiet and poorly resonant voice output, were an expression of his search for identity with regard to his role as a man.

A symptom may have very different meanings. Voice production that is too loud may denote self-assertion, hiding weakness or insecurity, and so on.

What becomes obvious is that it is only by means of searching with the client that the individual meaning of a symptom can be recognised. A symptom cannot simply be interpreted by the therapist alone.

From Person to Voice Function

As is the case with all methods of voice therapy or voice development, PVT is also a practical procedure. It is therefore not an alternative therapy. Standard exercises are used, but they are placed into a different context. This means that different practical procedures can be integrated, provided the basic principle that PVT is a person-oriented and not a function-oriented approach is taken into consideration.

> **All work on the voice**
> **must be instigated by the person concerned.**

This work has two aspects:

1. The needs of clients are of paramount importance.

   The goals set by the therapists are a proposal for the client and base themselves on physiological vocal production. However, what is decisive is what the clients wish to achieve for themselves.

   What may be considered to be a purposeful aim as far as therapy is concerned could, for example, be the clients' training their shouting voice. If, however, it is not possible to convince the clients of the necessity of this exercise, they will either refuse to do it or just play along like an obedient school child. This means that the work on their voices does not come from themselves, but from the therapist, who wants something for the clients because the therapist apparently knows what is good for them.

   The needs of the client are not only taken into general consideration, but influence the content of each individual sitting. This means that the therapist's planning is of secondary importance and that what is decisive is what the clients 'bring with them today'.

2. The voice function is developed in a person-oriented way.

   The structure of a (new) physiological voice function requires a certain systematic method, one that results from the functional process. The therapist can proceed along tried and tested exercise paths. There are two different practice paths: 'learning from the outside' or 'learning from the inside'.

Learning from the outside entails the therapist assigning exercises based on a normative exercise path and intervening to correct the clients if they deviate from the path. In this case the therapist decides what is correct and what is incorrect.

Learning from the inside is characterised by searching and testing different possibilities. Although the therapist offers suggestions, the search is always performed by the person concerned. This process of action is based on the belief that clients are, in principle, capable of satisfactory physiological voice functionality. However, in most cases it is hidden or confused. Through experimentation introduced by the therapist the attempt is made to develop the voice. The therapist needs to be just as creative as the client.

Learning from the inside also involves bringing the clients' power of imagination into play. Clients are encouraged to visualise functional processes, for example, to link them with pictorial images. The effect of the imagination is explained in more detail in Chapter 2.

Incorporating the clients' personal powers of imagination into therapy also means that the path is trodden by the clients. The therapist may offer suggestions that help stimulate the clients' imagination, but what the clients do in fact imagine is independent of the therapist and cannot be duplicated by the therapist. The clients tread their own inner path in order to bring about change.

The First Step into Person-oriented Voice Work

Work on the voice commences with the investigation of the anamnesis, the history of an illness (Greek *anamnesis* = remembering). This is a vital part of diagnosis and offers clues about the functional causes of the vocal disorder. In this initial conversation the clients are also asked about their motives for seeking treatment. This applies to clients who have no illness but would like to develop their voices.

Over and above recording the usual anamnesis data, PVT is concerned with preparing the ground for personal work. The attempt is made to instigate a process that induces the clients to question underlying reasons for their voice disorder. Their attention is turned towards making links which they have hitherto not recognised.

Evidence shows that ticking off individual questions on an anamnesis questionnaire one by one is fruitless. Only through a genuine conversation in which questions arise naturally are clients prepared to volunteer information about certain experiences. Apart from being aware of the content of what has been said, the therapist should take note of the way in which something has been described and of how the voice reacts in the process. This is an essential part of the examination.

What happens if the individual questions of an anamnesis questionnaire are dealt with one by one and in quick succession is that the person being questioned offers less emotional input, something that can lead to an incorrect diagnosis. After the anamnesis questionnaire the examiner may have gathered many facts, but will have been unable to discover what is really important.

The first step into person-oriented work should be taken with the utmost care, so that the clients are not overtaxed at this initial stage of treatment. Generally, clients only perceive their voice disorder as a disturbed function. This means that they expect a doctor to be able to help them by prescribing medication or measures to be taken, for example, inhaling. Instead the doctor has referred them for speech therapy, explaining that they are using their voices incorrectly. What they now expect are special voice exercises, which is in fact what they receive. But the idea that they should also ask themselves what the voice disorder has to do with their own selves is often something that is quite alien to them.

The process which should be initiated in the first sitting and which runs through the entire treatment is comprised of the following points:

- activating self-reflection
- understanding what the voice wants to say
- taking charge and adopting responsibility for one's own treatment.

Embarking on Self-reflection

An example:

A client goes into treatment because of the following complaint: her voice is slightly hoarse, very soft and tires very quickly.

When the anamnesis is investigated, it is discovered that her complaints followed an illness involving an infection, which she had experienced six months previously. Moving on to the level of personality, the client is asked whether she can remember the situation she found herself in when she was ill. She tells the therapist that she had a lot of work at the time and that her mother had also had an operation for cancer, which meant she did not really have enough time to recover properly from a cold.

When she is asked how her mother was at the time, the client responds that every time she was with her mother and she discovered that she was repressing her illness she 'felt choked'.

It would now be premature to conclude that this client is suffering from a psychogenic voice disorder or even that the need for psychotherapy is indicated. To begin with, the only concern is to have her understand that the voice is not only a function, but is also something that has to do with herself.

She has already pointed to the link between psyche and voice function by stating 'something made her feel choked'. She now needs to be made aware of the link.

In this example, asking her the question about the circumstances of her situation at the time the disorder occurred was the first decisive step on a personal level which enabled the client to introduce the subject of her mother's cancer.

The willingness on the part of the therapist to work on the personal level has the following effect on the clients:

1. The clients sense that interest is being shown in them as people, which represents an important factor in the relationship between client and therapist.
2. The clients receive the signal that their problems are not only justified, but constitute part of the therapy within the framework of the therapy.

The following offers an indication of the kind of personal aspects that typical questions may contain. For reasons mentioned earlier, the questions are not fully formulated.

Why start therapy now?
Particularly in the case of long-term complaints, this question may reveal information about any connection between an acute mental trauma or one that has got worse and the person's current situation.

When did the voice disorder become noticeable for the first time?
This may point to a concrete experience that triggered off the voice problems.

Do the complaints arise in particular situations or in the presence of certain people?
What is investigated is:

- Whether the voice sounds different at particular ***times of the day*** (connection with mood swings).
- Whether the voice causes problems in particular ***situations*** (excitement, stress).
- Whether a connection exists between ***state of mind*** and the voice (when 'wound up' or when having 'a bad hair day').
- Whether the voice changes in conversation with ***specific people*** (partner, parents, boss).
- Whether there are situations in which it becomes particularly ***annoying*** that the voice is not as it should be (demands made of oneself/indication of a dependency on specific people or situations of which the client is unaware).

When looking into all this, many clients are amazed at all the things that are to be included, and they require an explanation about the link between voice and self (see Chapter 1). Most people have at some time experienced situations in which their voices have failed them on account of their psychological state. It is therefore easy to convince them of the link between voice and self. On this basis they can also be convinced that treatment is only meaningful if these connections are incorporated into therapy.

The process of analysis starts with the initial conversation but extends far beyond it and runs through the whole treatment.

Understanding What the Voice Wants to Say

Example:

A patient who attempts to speak but cannot make a sound and is diagnosed as having 'psychogenic aphonia' attributes her problems to a goitre operation despite their having arisen quite some time after the operation. She suspects a further possible cause for her voice disorder to be a hereditary disposition, since her father always had a hoarse voice.

When the anamnesis is investigated, the patient is asked about when her illness started. She answers quite spontaneously that she can remember exactly when she first lost her voice. In the course of a long car journey with her fiancé she suddenly found that she could not converse with him any more. When she was asked what the conversa-

tion was about, she remembered that her fiancé had asked her when she would at last be prepared to get married.

This is pretty much a classic example of how our bodies (in this case our voices) can help us in putting off decisions. After losing her voice, this patient's wedding plans were no longer an issue: the bride was now ill and would at most have been able to whisper the eagerly awaited 'yes' word. By asking detailed questions on location, time and circumstances that accompanied this loss of voice the client began to think about it all and started to analyse her voice disorder.

A further example:

A 56-year-old teacher who usually has a rasping, hoarse voice (hyperfunctional dysphonia) has a remarkably melodious voice when he is invited to simulate his teaching situation. The conclusion that his problems were not triggered off by his professional practice, but that there must be another reason for them, seems reasonable.

In conversation it turns out that the client loves his job and gives his all in class. But after school he is completely exhausted and really just wants peace and quiet. Given the choice he would like to retire with a book. His wife, however, who is now no longer fully occupied because the children have left home, demands that they organise their leisure time together. Because she likes being in the company of other people she organises a busy social programme. Until now, the teacher has not realised that a conflict exists between his needs and those of his wife, which are equally justified. In this conflict his voice has reacted by showing symptoms such as hoarseness and strain, allowing him to disengage. Although he manages to gain his desired peace, he has to pay a high price for it.

This example shows how important it is for the voice therapist to analyse symptoms and not to draw premature conclusions. In the case of a teacher (a professional speaker) it would be more obvious to think of a voice disorder as being associated with his profession.

The goal of 'understanding what the voice wants to say' applies to both voice therapist and client. The search for the meaning of the symptom, conducted by the therapist, creates or increases the willingness of the clients to do the same thing and begin their search.

Again and again it is impressive to experience how the voice can spontaneously change as soon as the client shows willingness to understand what the voice wants to say, even before any kind of exercise has been conducted.

Taking Charge and Responsibility for One's Own Treatment

When clients begin to view their voice problems in connection with their selves it becomes obvious that changes in voice will have a consequence for the person as a whole. The decision to get involved in this process and to take responsibility for it lies with the client. The course the treatment takes is also influenced by it. The clients take charge so that they can find their own individual way of overcoming their problems. They themselves must show where they want to go, when they want to continue and when not, and how far they want to proceed. The effects this has on the relationship of therapist and client are described in more detail later in this chapter.

Assuming that a successful relationship that enables the clients to speak openly about themselves has been established with the clients in the first therapy session, it is recommended that the therapist go over the kind of changes it is hoped will be achieved from speech therapy again at the end of the sitting.

Surprisingly enough, these desires often exceed the actual concern about the voice. Clients who originally 'only' went into treatment because of physical voice complaints formulate therapy goals for themselves such as the following (examples from our practice):

'I want to learn how to express myself convincingly.'
'My voice should not be so timid, I feel inferior enough as it is.'
'I want to get rid of this feeling that I'm wearing a paper bag over my head, a feeling that I experience when stress kicks in. My voice sounds as if it is somewhere far away.'
'I want to have the voice that belongs to me.'

When therapy is started a written record should be made of these statements made by the clients along with a mental note to turn to them at the end of the treatment to see what became of their original concerns. Experience shows that sometimes problems that existed when treatment began disappear to such an extent that the clients later do not remember having ever had them. When they are put before them again, many people realise that they have taken a great step in personal development (compare pp. 28–30).

The Functional and Personal(ity) Levels of Voice Therapy Exercises

As already stated, voice therapy is mainly a practical process. The term 'voice exercise treatment' is also widely used by doctors.

PVT also exercises and trains the voice function, but the tonal result of the produced or practised tone is not what is most important, it directs its attention towards the actual process of practising and towards the person who practises.

This is why there are two levels in PVT that are distinguished from one another: the functional level and the personal level.

Functional Level

What is meant by the functional level is the carrying out of an exercise and with it the acquisition of a physiological voice function. Voice therapists must have sound knowledge of the anatomical and physiological aspects of the voice organ and the components involved in vocal production, that is, tonus, breathing, and so on. Experiences with one's own voice are insufficient to qualify one for treating the vocal disorder of another person. Lack of knowledge with regard to physiological context can lead to the wrong exercises being suggested. This becomes apparent from the example of the acquisition of the 'support'.

The aim of the support is to counteract the air's being breathed out too rapidly and forcefully while producing a sound. The increased tension in the diaphragm necessary for this is often achieved by further training of tension in the abdominal muscles. Instead of activating the diaphragm itself in order to restrain air, the attempt is made to achieve this by fixing the abdominal muscles in a position. 'Dosage' is here mistaken with 'holding'. Holding is, however, not consistent with physiological breathing and vocal production.

Particularly in the case of organic dysphonia, an exact knowledge of the anatomy and physiology of voice production is imperative.

If there is existing damage to the organs involved in vocal production the aim is to work on achieving the best possible strategies for compensating for the disturbed function. In this case 'functional work' is of great importance.

'Functional voice training' (Rohmert, 1991) demonstrates the connections between particular movements, muscle activities and functions of the larynx. Voice therapists are advised to check the catalogues of methods they have, which have been handed down over the years, and to make sure that they are up to date.

In PVT it is very important that therapists, apart from possessing vital technical competence, are able to explain the functional level of exercises to clients. This is described in detail on pp. 25–27.

Personal Level

On the personal level all feelings and thoughts that become apparent during exercises with clients are recorded. The purpose of this is not for the therapist to interpret and evaluate them, but to encourage the clients to increase their awareness and express their feelings through questioning. This often enables the clients to understand their 'inner' processes and typical behaviour patterns that result from them. Vocal production is also a part of this.

Intense work on the frontal position of sound (compare Part III), for example, may constitute a step on a functional level that can be taken quickly. However, if, on a personal level, the client understands the context as one where the frontal position of sound has something to do with 'getting to the front' or 'stepping outside of oneself', the steps will probably be taken more slowly because they will be taken more carefully.

The link between the functional and personal level of voice therapy should become clearer through the following example:

Through achieving a proportioning of breathing that is most appropriate for individual speaking (Breath Rhythm Timed Phonation according to Coblenzer and Muhar, 1976) clients are able to increase the amount of air they take in well (are able to 'relax') and proportion their speech phrases well in a practice situation.

However, when speaking spontaneously they are not able to do this, since they are unable to allow themselves to take the pauses for breath that would allow them reflexly to complete the intake of air. It is unlikely that they will learn through practice alone the technique of 'letting air flow back in' used when talking.

These patients first need to understand what causes them to disregard the necessary breathing pauses. There may be various reasons behind this, for example, the fear of taking up too much space and therefore the feeling that one therefore has to be quick. Or the exact opposite, the feeling of not having enough space and of therefore having to cram as much as possible into the time available. It could also be the fear of losing the thread or the desire to be as precise as possible, leading to linguistic overproduction, or in fact a whole host of other reasons.

This example shows how a particular symptom, which in different people may be very similar on a functional level, can have completely different causes on a personal level. By looking into the different reactions of clients, each course of vocal therapy, despite the similar exercises, becomes a completely individual process of action. When the clients understand what lies behind their linguistic or vocal behaviour the practising of a certain function gains a further dimension. In our example, practising economical breathing phonation can lead to the testing and practising of a new behaviour pattern 'allowing oneself more pauses'. By working on rhythm of breath it may be possible to bring about a change in the rhythm of life. Self-perception becomes self-experience in PVT with regard to the psychophysical-mental unity of the person.

Concentrated Work on the Body as a Basis of PVT

Functional and Personal Meaning of Work on the Body

The voice function is movement and like any movement is dependent on the tonus (tension situation) of muscles. The laryngeal area cannot be viewed in isolation. Its tonus depends on the tonus of the entire body. If this is too low or too high it will not be possible to achieve optimal performance (compare Part II).

What is necessary is what is called 'eutonus'. This word stems from the Greek and literally means 'good (*eu*) tension (*tonus*)' (see Alexander, 1992: 25).

As a result of the functional association between voice function and muscle tonus, work on the voice should always be linked to work on tension throughout the whole body. Two significant directions have been developed in voice therapy with a view to influencing body tension, the objective of which is to achieve eutonus:

1. Work on the body by means of movement. This includes gymnastic exercises and active loosening-up exercises.
2. Work on the body by means of bodily self-perception.

Methods that operate via bodily self-perception (proprioception) and may be grouped under the concept 'concentrative body work' (Madelung, 1987) are, among others:

Eutonie after Gerda Alexander
Feldenkrais method
Alexander technique
Breathing work after Ilse Middendorf
Breathing meditation after Hetty Draayer.

The objective of these methods extends beyond the regulation of bodily processes and sees work on the body as a possible way of working on the person as a whole as well as of working on his or her physical, emotional, mental and spiritual potential. These methods operate on the assumption that specific tensions within the body have a 'personal side' to them.

To quote J. Kriz:

> Any kind of stress, be it of a mental or of a physical nature (here too a division is arbitrary), causes bodily tension that usually disappears once the stress has been eliminated. However, in the case of long-term stress (for example unresolved emotional conflict, the constant frustration of important needs etc.) these tensions become chronic – they find expression in muscular tension ... Tensions therefore stem from each specific emotional conflict or other protracted strains that have been experienced in the course of life. As the muscular system simultaneously determines posture, this means that such characteristic tensions result in typical 'character stances' that in turn result in a particular kind of experience and conduct (e.g. a tensed muscle denies the possibility of deeper breathing and, by so doing, that of experiencing intense feelings and sadness). (1991: 94)

Such a reading of the connection between body and psyche almost rules out work on the body as a primary objective of correction and functional improvement. Therefore with PVT, concerned as it is with complete treatment, concentrative work on the body occupies a central position.

Proprioception and Imagination

As explained on pp. 8–10, PVT is based on the conviction that change is something that should occur consciously. Perception plays a decisive role, for without perception conscious change is not possible. Training bodily self-perception, proprioception, is therefore the basis upon which all work on breathing and voice function is built.

Among other things, proprioception is the ability to perceive oneself. It concerns deep sensitivity, position in space and position of joints in relation to one another. Secondly, it harbours a creative potential within itself since we are able to react to what we perceive of ourselves. Madelung (1987) distinguishes two principles:

Principle A: Pure perception as potential agent of change

If, for example, we direct our concentration to the soles of our feet and perceive how they touch the floor, a change in our muscle tonus occurs. This means that through perception alone, changes occur of their own accord.

Principle B: Imagination as potential agent of change

Another possibility is consciously to further body perception through the use of visual images.

We can go further than perceiving our feet as described above and 'see into' the interior of the foot in our imagination. For example, we can imagine that more space is created or that our toes get longer or roots grow from our feet into the ground.

We can influence our condition depending on the direction we allow our perception to take when linking it to an image.

Ultimately the two principles are inseparable. 'Pure perception' is itself already linked to an image that stems from our experience, in our example an image of the foot. The difference between Principle A and Principle B is that with Principle A an image is consciously combined with perception.

The most recent neurophysiological research proceeds on the assumption not only that perception and imagination are linked, but also that a reciprocal action occurs between them. This forms the basis for, among other things, mental training in high-performance sports and therapy approaches in psychosomatic medicine (Simonton et al., 1980).

Substance and Objectives of Work on the Body in PVT

The origins of the various methods of concentrative work on the body that are used for work on the body in PVT are to be found in the experiences we, the two authors of this book, have ourselves had. The individual methods place emphasis on different focal points. The notion they have in common is that of the inseparability of body, soul and spirit.

Elements have been taken over or modified for voice therapy that are appropriate for fulfilling the speech therapist's task: to improve the function of vocal production.

The focal points of work on the body in PVT are:

- bodily self-perception (proprioception)
- regulating of tonus
- centring.

1. Bodily self-perception (proprioception).
   The therapy begins with the teaching of bodily self-perception, which simultaneously forms the basis and starting point for every further exercise in the course of treatment. PVT differs from other kinds of voice therapy methods in that bodily self-perception is given priority, which means that work is primarily conducted via the channel of kinaesthetic perception and less via auditory perception. Even if it is possible to influence the production of sound by means of the control of the sound of the voice, and in individual cases it can be necessary and helpful, we have the following reasons for our general procedure:
   In situations with a high level of noise (for example, in a restaurant or while travelling in a car) a differentiated perception of the sound of one's own voice is hardly possible. It is precisely situations such as these that prove to put extreme strain on many people's voices. As a rule these situations lead to voice strain or tense posture. These bodily symptoms can be perceived via the kinaesthetic channel, making a correction of voice behaviour easier than it would be via hearing.
   What further complicates control of the sound of the voice via hearing, apart from this, is that one's own voice is perceived not only via the ear canal, but also via bone conduction. We hear our own voice differently from the way other people hear it. This may lead to a vocal behaviour that has negative consequences. Increasing tension in the vocal tract, for example, may give the speaker the auditory impression that his or her voice has more brilliance. However, to the listener it just sounds more metallic and strained. Furthermore, prolonged increased exertion will have consequences for the vocal organ.
   The reason why the teaching of bodily self-perception in PVT plays such an important role, apart from the reasons mentioned above, is that it makes direct access on a personal level possible.
2. Regulating of tonus.
   Through working on the body, clients can learn that the regulation of tonus, which usually happens involuntarily, can be directed consciously. The gamma nervous system, which regulates the required tonus for the respective muscular activity,

and which can be influenced by directing our attention to our body, makes this possible. The desired eutonus as ideal condition for every motion, hence also for voice function, is made possible on a voluntary basis (compare Part II).

A state of tonus that is balanced and flexible is, however, not only important as far as it concerns muscle activity in the area of vocal production, but has repercussions for our whole being. As our 'psychotonus' (for example, extreme agitation or depression) has a strong influence on the tonus of the muscular system, the same applies in reverse: if the tonus of the muscle system is balanced we are also psychologically balanced.

The result is that vocal exercises only become effective once the physical and the psychological requirements have been met by means of a regulation of tonus, so that the voice can develop with ease.

3. Centring.

Centring means concentrating on the core of the body, the middle of the body. The core is located in the abdominal-pelvic region below the navel and is given various names: centre, middle, base area, root area, vital area, and so on.

The concept of centring is the basis of many Eastern doctrines and types of combat sports, such as aikido, yoga and tai chi, to name but a few, and also of zen meditation. What all these have in common is that energy is centred and operates in the pelvis.

Centring is also very significant for vocal production from both a functional and a personal perspective. The better the anchorage in the foundation of the body, the easier it will be for the voice to develop. To draw a comparison with a tree: the more deeply and securely it is rooted in the earth, the easier it is for its branches to move without the danger of the tree toppling over.

When applied to physiological processes, anchorage in depth means:

- the diaphragm is able to sink – breathing becomes deeper, and the necessary condition for supportive breathing, which is understood as 'elastic tension', is brought about
- The sinking of the diaphragm causes the larynx to be pulled downwards – the vocal cords are relaxed and can vibrate with more ease

- the centre of gravity is shifted from the upper to the lower half of the body, which causes a relieving of tension in the shoulder/neck and laryngeal areas.

In conjunction with discovering the physical effect of centring, people who practise it quickly come to feel the effect it has on their psychological state. 'One is no longer thrown off balance so easily', neither bodily nor mentally.

If one considers how dependent the voice is on emotional arousal it becomes clear why PVT places so much importance on centring.

Concentrative work on the body is the basis of PVT. It is not an isolated part of the therapy, but has a close connection to work on the voice. It forms part of the initial therapy session and continues to run through the whole treatment. This means that any further exercise on breathing, voice and articulation begins with bodily self-perception, regulating of tonus and centring.

The Relationship between Therapist and Client in PVT

So far we have described how PVT addresses the personal level of clients. Here we address the personal level of the therapists and ther-apeutical attitude in PVT. Apart from the basic idea of 'voice function to person – person to voice function', the therapist as a person and his or her relationship with the client is of central importance in PVT.

The Therapist as a Person

Functional vocal disorders, unlike organic vocal disorders or linguistic and speech disorders, are symptoms that therapists experience like everybody else. To have a frog in one's throat, a shaky voice, to hold one's breath; what therapist is not familiar with these things? This fact shows the extent to which a voice can be functionally unstable if a disorder arises on a personal level. If this were not the case then all voice therapists would have 'flawless' voices, which is evidently not true (one would almost say fortu-nately) going by conferences and further development courses. What this means is that therapists are more easily able to understand the problems of clients. Yet clarity, ability to reflect and being able to view the problems from a distance despite the closeness brought about through therapeutic work, is essential. It would be a huge mistake to project experiences with one's own voice on to the clients.

PVT requires that therapists show their willingness to open themselves up. The more sensitised clients are to bodily processes and symptoms and their connection with the self, the more capable they are of perceiving the posture, breathing, jaw expanse, and so on, of therapists.

Voice therapists need to be able to walk a tightrope. On the one hand, they should not give up their role as therapist and make their own problems the subject of conversation. On the other hand, they should not feign inappropriate 'superiority' but be a model to the clients in the way that they use their own voice.

This is the point at which the necessity for personal (vocal) experience and the readiness to supervise arise. In the role of the voice therapist, both serve to improve the ability to reflect.

The Therapist as Method

The phenomenon that voice therapists themselves become part of the method they use is a further particularity of voice therapy. The inner attitude of the therapist, which may, for example, be sensed by the client, will be a factor in the question of whether the client feels him- or herself corrected on a functional level or feels 'touched' as a person. The therapist must be clear about the 'quality' of his or her contact with the client. If, for example, the therapist's main objective is the straightening out of the vocal tract (compare Chapter 6) in order to bring about improved tone, the 'correction' of head posture would be contact that occurs on a functional level. This 'contact' may be compared to having your hair cut at the hairdressers, because it is similarly objective-oriented. Contact is realised in PVT when the therapist is open to any kind of reaction on the client's part and when he or she assumes an attitude of support, accompaniment and genuine inner contact with the client.

The Relationship between Therapist and Client

The same principle that applies to other types of therapy is also applicable when a voice patient seeks the help of a voice therapist:

The patient expects the therapist to show the recognition, empathy and ability that will alleviate their suffering. With regard to professional competence, there is an implied understanding of the asymmetry of the relationship. It is the therapist's responsibility to ensure that this does not turn into an acceptance and confirmation of asymmetry. (Bay, 1991: 81)

In other words, voice therapists are not superior to clients just because they are 'better' acquainted with the voice. This is why it is important that therapists reflect upon their relationship to their clients, if necessary with the help of supervision.

Transactional analysis (Berne, 1982) presents a model that describes the condition of the self and provides us with a good means with which to try to understand the level (parents–self, adults–self, child–self) on which client and patient are operating. At the same time it may serve to clarify their interaction and communication.

A voice disorder is a communication disturbance. This is why the type of communication that exists between therapist and client plays a decisive role for diagnosis and treatment of the disorder.

If, for example, a client speaks in a 'squeaky', childlike voice, the effect this has is to force his or her opposite into the role of parent. Working on chest and body resonance should enable the client to confront his or her opposite with a tone of conviction that places him or her on the level of an adult.

What may be determined for the first time in a therapy session and may serve as a exemplary model is whether and to what extent a client successfully achieves a new (vocal) behaviour pattern. The client is also given the opportunity of experiencing how his or her opposite (the therapist) reacts to this behaviour.

A male youth with mutational falsetto provides a clear example. Seen from a functional perspective, the task of lowering too high a voice pitch is a big problem for neither client nor therapist. The difficulty of this disturbance lies in the client's accepting the adult and male role that is linked to the deep voice. Providing the client with honest and credible feedback on an adult level will therefore be of great importance for the stabilisation and long-term use of a low voice register (Eberle, 1979).

Consequences for Therapeutical Work on the Voice

Transparency of therapy is an important requirement for the therapist and client being able to meet on an adult level. The clients must always have every exercise and all the content of the treatment explained to them so that they can decide whether to take particular steps in the therapy or not. In the example just presented the boy plays a role in the decision when he tries out the lower voice register for the first time.

If the therapist makes the effort to ensure transparency by providing clear information about the physiological contexts and providing precise explanations of the effects of particular methods, he or she will thereby take the pressure off the client who will then be in a position to participate responsibly and actively in shaping the form the therapy takes. This can only be done on the condition that the therapist relinquish his or her position of superiority as therapist. The client is now able to be creative: he or she can experiment with the voice and with his or her own self. He or she can now learn to develop his or her own individual exercise programme and vocal aids. This is how self-determined action on the part of the client is brought about in therapy, which is also an important requirement for the client's being able to take responsibility for him- or herself outside therapy. A real curing of a symptom (not the shifting of a symptom), as is the case in personality development, cannot be effected on an external level by another person. We have now touched on the subject of transfer, which we are going to deal with in greater detail below.

Transfer as a Consciously Executed, Permanent Process of Change

The Problem of Transfer

Transfer – the act of conveying the newly acquired vocal pattern into everyday language – is the main problem that voice therapy has to contend with.

Towards the end of treatment the number of exercises designed to facilitate this transfer are increased. Possibilities are: reading aloud, describing pictures, and conversations in which the voice is perceived by client as well as therapist. What may effectively be achieved in these exercises may, however, often not be realisable in everyday language no matter how intensively practised: the old vocal pattern stubbornly persists. Time and again the well practised function is interfered with by personal factors. The practising of the function only fulfils a necessary, but not yet sufficient, requirement for a change. When transfer genuinely succeeds, a change in attitude and behaviour occurs. This process may occur unconsciously or be carried out consciously. Most of the time it must occur consciously, that is, it only becomes possible if the client decides in favour of it and all the consequences that may arise from it.

Example:

A 32-year-old client finds that she can no longer identify with her high-pitched, childlike voice and visits a group, 'Voice Development'. She has heard 'that something can be done there'.

She quickly succeeds in finding her adult female voice: a warm, richly resonant and deep voice, about which she herself and the group are enthusiastic. Her husband on the other hand is not. She married a much older man when she was 21 who now cannot accept the new vocal pattern of his wife. The client feels much more self-confident with her 'new' voice, which seems to frighten her husband. In order for her to transfer this new vocal pattern into everyday language it is necessary for her to resolve this conflict with her partner, but her husband is not prepared to do this. He sticks to his opinion that the new voice is unfeminine and indirectly warns of the consequences it will have for their relationship.

The client finally leaves the group, fully conscious of the fact that she now knows her voice, but does not (yet) possess enough courage to assert herself with it.

Transfer as a Process of Behavioural Change

It is one of PVT's main objectives to convey clearly that transfer is seen as a permanent process, for which clients must consciously decide. This takes away the clients' frequent illusion that their voices will somehow improve through what the therapists 'do with them', without they themselves having to change. During treatment it must be made clear to the clients that the therapists are unable to take the steps towards changing the clients' voices on their behalf. However, this does not by any means signify that the clients are left on their own to deal with the problem of transfer.

On the contrary: PVT aims to provide continual support so that they can achieve a real transfer. This is effected by providing appropriately devised exercises at the end of treatment and by supporting the clients on their path of change (compare Chapter 10). Consequently, transfer logically commences with treatment. From the very beginning of treatment, therapists and clients continually consider which alternative learned behaviour might be suitable for integration into everyday life. What is most easy to integrate is what has been achieved in the area of tonus/posture, which often leads to a noticeable improvement of the voice at the beginning of the treatment.

Clarity about the question of transfer also helps in deciding when a treatment should end. In this way the clients can be prevented from trying to prolong treatment for the purpose of enjoying the agreeable exercises and the attention of the therapists, without taking on any responsibility for themselves and their treatment. The treatment is concluded when the clients have experienced enough improvement to enable them to get on with their voice on their own.

Voice Awareness as the Objective of Vocal Work

The process of voice development extends beyond the treatment. Through therapy the client gains vocal awareness. The voice becomes a friend that accompanies a person on the path of self-development. Like a seismograph, the voice can be an early indicator of whether something is wrong, since the body and its functions can often tell us more than our heads.

What applies in principle is: 'Situations that are not good for my voice are not good for me.'

In situations where the voice becomes peculiar, an inner dialogue could be conducted with the voice, running along the lines of:

What does my voice sound like?
(harsh, whining, forced, and so on)

What is the situation?
(conversation with boss, partner, and so on)

What is the problem that lies behind this situation?
(fear of confrontation, fear of weakness, and so on)

Can I influence the situation?
(changing the location of conversation, postponing the conversation to a more convenient time)

Can I alter my attitude?
(processing fears)

Can I behave differently?
(alter my frame of mind by changing my sitting posture, conscious use of new vocal pattern)

We must rid ourselves of the illusion that our voice is always 'OK'. We do not always function how we would like to as a person, and in the same way our voice also differs. Our voice is not only part of us, we 'are' our voice. It offers itself as an instrument for self-awareness because it leads to increased consciousness by means of vocal consciousness.

Like all problems, voice problems have a positive side to them. They are challenges and opportunities for getting to grips with processes of growth and maturation.

Big problems in life are never permanently solved. If they are apparently so, then it is always a loss. Their meaning and purpose does not appear to lie in their resolution, but in that we unremittingly work on them. This alone saves us from stupefaction and fossilisation. (Jung, 1990: 68)

Part II
Anatomical and Physiological Aspects Seen From Functional and Personal Perspectives

As explained in Chapter 2, transparent therapy content plays an important role in PVT. This includes client knowledge about anatomical and physiological links in vocal production. The following chapters are designed to show how PVT attempts to explain complicated processes such as vocal fold vibration or concepts like 'Breath Rhythm Timed Phonation' (Coblenzer and Muhar, 1976) so that they can be made intelligible to clients. These descriptions are often pictorial explanations that incorporate client experiences and knowledge into what is to be newly learnt.

We are less concerned with an anatomically/physiologically absolutely precise representation of the process of phonation. This information can be found in some specialised ENT and phonology books. We are more concerned with proceeding with a vivid method of explanation, one that is based upon the interests and existing knowledge of clients and conveys the clearest possible idea of voice production.

Apart from the descriptions designed to provide better under-standing of vocal production, there are little 'excursions' in the individual chapters. They lead from the functional level to a level that considers the bodily functions from an overall aspect, thereby indicating the further path to the personal level of voice function.

3
Outline

Figure 3.1 gives an outline of the organs and functions involved in voice production. Included are breathing (3), the utterance of vocal sounds (phonation) (2), and the formation of speech sounds (articulation) (1).

A further component important for voice production is body tension (tonus). It influences and is influenced by posture and intention. By intention we mean the intended expression and expressive behaviour that adapts to a particular situation.

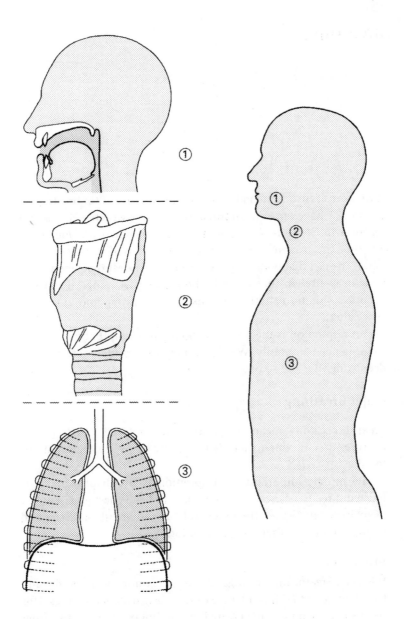

Figure 3.1

4
Breathing

If we were to hear somebody say the words 'I gasped for breath', we would not have enough information to know whether the bodily reaction to exertion (for example, climbing stairs) was meant or whether the person concerned had just received some shocking news. The fact that both are possible reflects the fact that when body tension is altered, that is, when bodily or psychological tension occurs, respiration rhythm, intensity of breathing and breathing space alter.

Our respiration is the only vital bodily function that we are able to influence voluntarily. We can consciously breathe more rapidly, deeply, lightly, and so on.

Quiet Breathing

Breathing calmly means inspiration in a relaxed situation and posture, that is, when there is no bodily or psychological strain involved.

The muscle important for respiration is the diaphragm. It is located directly between the abdomen and the chest area. Further respiratory muscles are the inner and outer intercostal muscles and a series of muscles that assist respiration.

Inspiration

When we breathe in, the lungs take in air, causing the ribs to rise and the diaphragm to sink, and increasing the capacity of the lungs. This results in a vacuum being created in the thorax, allowing the lungs to fill with air (Figure 4.1).

If the diaphragm is lowered by a centimetre the result is an intake of 300 ml of air. Breathing is therefore a reaction to movement.

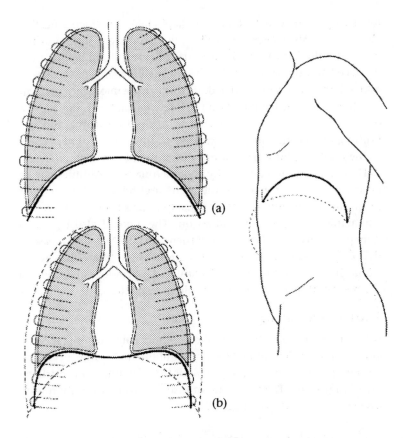

Figure 4.1: Position of the diaphragm during inspiration (a) and expiration (b)

Expiration

When we breathe out, the diaphragm relaxes and curves upwards, and in so doing assumes its starting position. The ribs sink and the elastic restoring forces of the lungs cause them to be pumped more or less empty. The breathing path runs from the lungs via the bronchi into the windpipe. From there it runs through the larynx to the throat and out through the mouth or nose, and vice versa. Calm breathing is conducted through the nose.

Abdomen-Flanks Breathing

According to which muscles are stronger, a distinction is drawn between shallow breathing and abdomen-flanks breathing. As the latter form of breathing is physiological it is the one that is aimed for. This process requires a flexible diaphragm, for which a flexible abdominal wall is necessary. When the diaphragm sinks and the lungs are filled with air, the internal organs that lie below it are displaced and the abdominal wall is pushed forward. If movement of the diaphragm is unrestricted, this will create maximum space in the thorax and the basal parts of the lungs will also be supplied with oxygen. This can also be referred to as deep breathing and has nothing to do with pumping excessive air into oneself. 'Deep' refers to the location of the air breathed rather than to its volume.

There are several reasons why abdomen-flanks breathing may be obstructed: clothes may be too tight around the abdomen, or furniture may be uncomfortable, making one sit hunched over, or damaging one's posture, and so on. These could also be called 'functional' reasons. Beside these there are also 'personal' reasons that may cause us to strain our abdominal wall. 'Butterflies in the stomach' are often the result. Physical and psychological tension in the body both play an important role in respiration.

Rhythm of Breathing

Between expiration and inspiration a short pause takes place, the end of which is determined by a new impulse to breathe, occurring automatically. If no vocal production is intended, unrestricted breathing occurs. The time-ratio of inspiration and expiration is on average 1 : 1.5 (compare page 42).

> *We are familiar with rhythm from dance. Rhythms can be fast and slow, regular and irregular, catchy. It stands to reason that a whole evening of slow waltzing is boring and that after dancing to ten modern songs on the trot you will need a 'breather'. The more diverse the programme the easier it will be to keep on going.*

This picture of different rhythms can be transferred to breathing rhythms. If we observe and are conscious of them in different situations this can help us to see that breathing rhythm has something to do with the rhythm of life. How we handle pauses in breathing and speech may reflect the importance pauses have for our individual rhythms of life.

Speech Breathing

Speech breathing is the process of expiration during speech and inspiration during speech pauses.

The contribution made by Coblenzer and Muhar towards the problem of achieving a physiological state of breathing and vocal production – their essential work *Atem und Stimme* ('Breath and Voice') (1976) is an essential standard work in voice therapy. We have adopted concepts introduced by these authors in our explanations of speech breathing.

Valve Function of Voice and Articulation

In the act of speaking the vocal folds in the larynx vibrate when air is breathed out and a sound is thereby created (Chapter 5) that is formed into a speech sound through articulation (Chapter 6) in the mouth. The air is more or less sent through valves and measured out into proper doses.

A garden hose provides a good comparison of how these valves co-operate and air is breathed out.

When watering a tree we turn the tap as far as it will go and screw off the hose valve so that a lot of water flows with relatively little pressure. When cleaning the car the tap is turned just as far, but the jet is concentrated and the pressure increased because of the valve. When watering rose bushes we turn the tap just slightly and almost close the valve so that we create a gentle mist using very little water.

In this pictorial comparison the flowing water corresponds to air that is breathed out. The tap represents the diaphragm and hence the pressure of air, and the hose valve has a similar function to the valves, vocal folds and articulatory organs (compare Chapters 5 and 6).

Reflex Breath Completion

In order to be able to get your breath back during speech pauses it is important to relax the valve tension of the vocal cords or articulators and let go of the diaphragm at the end of a section of speech.

Coblenzer and Muhar (1976) lay great emphasis on 'Relaxation'. The vocal folds move apart creating an entry valve that is wide open for respiration. This means that inspiration occurs with little effort and cannot be heard. Air flows in in a reflex-like manner. This process is described as 'reflex breath completion'.

On a personal level the physiological processes of relaxation and reflex breath completion touch upon the subject of 'letting go'. Most people find this difficult and prefer to rely on active muscular activity to regain their breath, instead of trusting that the air will flow back of its own accord. Audible inspiration is therefore a sign of pathological breathing.

Breath Rhythm Timed Phonation

When speaking the time between inspiration and expiration rises from a ratio of 1 : 3 to a ratio of 1 : 8 (Wirth, 1995).

The pause in breathing which takes place in calm breathing is identical to the pause in speech breathing. Coblenzer and Muhar have measured that reflex breath completion can take place in 0.2 of a second. This seems quite incredible considering how many people one sees gasping for breath when speaking since they seem not to have léft themselves time to make the necessary pauses in speech. They gasp for breath following sections of speech that are too long by increasingly using the inspiration musculature of the thorax. By making the next phrase of speech so long they exhaust their air supply down to the last breath. They digress from the middle breathing position, the balanced relation of inspirational and expirational forces (see Figure 4.2c)

We are familiar with the personal aspect of 'exhausting oneself'.

It is not so much the punctuation marks or the contents of the texts, for example, of the spoken words, that should dictate speech pauses, but more the speaker's individual rhythm of breathing. Rhythm of breathing is influenced by physical and psychological tensions, the conversation situation, conversation partner(s) and the respective intention.

Dividing up speech phrases in accordance with one's own breathing leads to Breath Rhythm Timed Phonation.

Inspiratory Countertension during Phonation (Support)

The intention to speak causes the diaphragm to sink, and air consumption, which is 'programmed' by the brain, remains economical during the course of speaking. The diaphragm assumes the state it usually would during inspiration, although speaking occurs with exhalation. The result of this is that the air is released in a more restrained manner, minimising pressure and relieving the valve vocal folds.

Intention (Chapter 7) plays an important role in 'programming'. It is intention that causes the diaphragm to sink and that keeps it in its state of elastic breathhold. This tension is commonly known as 'support' and, apart from its being significant when discussing speech, it is of particular importance for singing (compare Chapter 13, pp. 183–189).

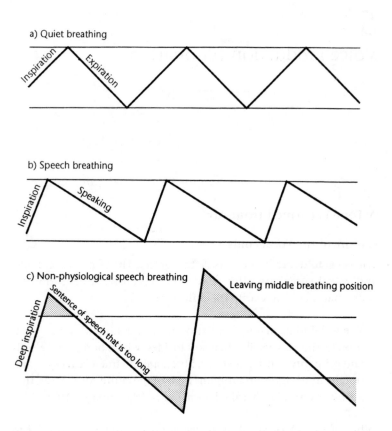

a) Quiet breathing

Inspiration

Expiration

b) Speech breathing

Inspiration

Speaking

c) Non-physiological speech breathing

Sentence of speech that is too long

Deep inspiration

Leaving middle breathing position

Figure 4.2: Schematic representation of different rhythms of breath

What should be kept in mind is that support is intentional, that is, it is controlled centrally and does not occur through a mechanical tightening of the abdominal muscles.

5
Voice Production (Phonation)

A Tone is Formed from Air

Closure of the Vocal Folds

The vocal folds are located inside the larynx. The terms 'vocal folds' and 'vocal cords' are often used synonymously. A definition by Habermann aims to clarify the difference:

> The vocal folds mainly consist of muscle, mainly of the ... vocal muscle, the M. vocalis. Their soft insides, which border the glottis and primarily consist of elastic fibres, are the true vocal cords and not the much more voluminous folds of the entire vocal cords, that are often erroneously called vocal cords. (Habermann, 1978: 33)

When we speak of vocal folds, we are using the word to refer to muscle, connective tissue and mucosal covering (Figure 5.1).

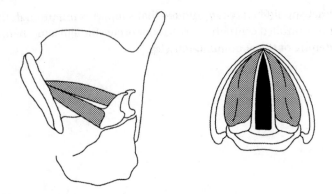

Figure 5.1: Schematic representation of vocal folds

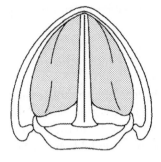
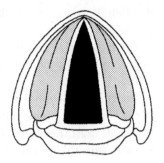

a: Position for vocal production   b: Respiration position

Figure 5.2: Position of vocal folds

If we wish to produce a tone when speaking or singing, the vocal folds that are wide open for breathing need to be closed. This means that the space between the vocal folds is closed. This space is known as the glottis.

A distinction is made between the breathing position of the vocal folds and the phonation position (position for vocal production) (Figure 5.2).

The process of closing the vocal folds becomes central, it is regulated by the brain. The adjustment of the vocal folds to the desired pitch through a change in tension, length and mass (compare pp. 47–48) is connected with this.

Vocal Fold Vibration

If you blow up a balloon and then let it go it whirls through the air and produces a whizzing noise.

If you hold the blown up balloon in your hand and pull the rubber, stretching it length-wise at the mouthpiece, a little slit appears through which air escapes.

You can hear a kind of whistling noise which can be altered depending on the extent to which you stretch the rubber length-wise. The air that escapes through the rubber slit (chink, glottal chink) has the capacity to produce sound.

Although this pictorial comparison may not be precise since the factors mentioned above, that is, the structure of the vocal folds and the flexibility of its mass, are also involved along with those of the pressure of the blown air and tension. It does, however, clearly illustrate how air sets an elastic something vibrating and thereby produces a sound.

The closed glottis is re-opened by the air that streams in from below, by the flexibly tensed vocal folds being more or less blown apart.

The glottis functions like a valve which, depending on the tension of the vocal cords, is closed more or less tightly. The pressure of the blown air must therefore adjust to this 'resistance'. Almost simultaneously with the opening of the glottis, the vocal folds are sucked together again.

The width of the windpipe, the narrowness of the glottal chink and the breadth of the throat are the main factors of the particular aerodynamics to which the flow of air is subject.

The following comparison is intended to clarify the effect this has:

In the foyer of a cinema the visitors are waiting to be admitted to the auditorium. The crowd of people waiting in front of the doors begins to pack together and people start jostling each other. As soon as their admission tickets are torn off, the people who are let through hurry along to secure the best seats.

Air molecules behave in a similar way to the cinema visitors. They gather below the glottis, eventually 'pressing' it open. If you now also visualise the cinema visitors all pressing up against one another (as the air molecules do) those that have just passed the entrance will force those behind to be pulled along with them.

Some of the air molecules also 'stick' to the walls, causing the flexible vocal folds and the mucosal covering that lies gently on top to be pulled along a little. In conjunction with the opening and closing action of the vocal folds, this causes the vocal folds to roll off against each other (see Figure 5.3).

It becomes clear that vocal fold vibration is a highly complex process, which consists fundamentally of three components:

- pressure of the blown air
- position and tension of the laryngeal muscles
- elasticity and condition of the vocal folds.

An unhindered interplay of these components leads to a precise process of vocal fold vibration and creates a clear sound as a result.

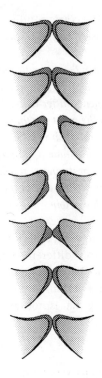

Figure 5.3: Roll-off action of the vocal folds' mucosal covering

This sound is also referred to as the primary laryngeal tone and governs the pitch and volume of sound.

Pitch

The opening, closing and roll-off action of the vocal folds are completed in very quick periodic changes: the vocal folds vibrate, a sound is produced.

The frequency of this vibration determines the pitch. The average frequency of a male voice lies between 90 and 130 vibrations per second (unit: hertz (Hz)). The average frequency of a female voice lies between 190 and 260 Hz. In musical terms this can be translated into notes: G to c or g to c^1. The middle speaking-voice register of men or women lies within these ranges. The complete vocal range of a healthy voice lies between two and three octaves.

Frequency of vibration is only one of the factors that determine pitch. Further factors are the length and the density of the vocal cords that are altered by the corresponding activity of the laryngeal muscles and thereby adjusted to the respective pitch.

The strings of a cello vary in length and strength from those of a violin. This is what determines the difference in pitch. The individual strings of the respective instruments differ as well, because of their varying strengths. Depending on the point at which the freely vibrating part of a string is gripped, a certain pitch will be produced. The tautness of a string can be varied, which is how it is tuned. Increasing the tautness of a string causes it to vibrate more quickly and the tone produced becomes higher. Easing it slightly causes the frequency of the vibration to decrease, producing a lower tone.

If you relate this example to vocal folds it becomes obvious how the pitch alters depending on different lengths, thicknesses and tensions. As a rule, the voice becomes higher when tension increases. It becomes obvious that a certain amount of tension is vital for vibration to occur. A string that is not taut or a vocal fold that has no tension cannot vibrate.

Volume

Volume is the second primary voice function of the larynx. Volume is produced by increasing the amplitude of vocal fold vibration. What is meant by amplitude is the extent of the vibration, which varies depending on the pressure of the air that is breathed out. The conclusion that follows is: the harder the air blows on the vocal folds, the louder the tone will be, but this is only conditional. If the air pressure were too great, the vocal cords would just be blown apart; the valve must be able to withstand the pressure. The principle of air dosage and support described in Chapter 4 is therefore also applicable in the case of very loud tones. Many people confuse volume with resonance.

Interfering Factors

There are a number of reasons why the primary laryngeal tone may be impaired, some of these being:

- defective function
- organic changes to the vocal folds
- interfering or damaging influences to the larynx.

Functional voice disorders are the main object of concern in this book. Organic voice disorders are discussed in detail in Part IV.

At this point we would like to mention the most common damaging influences that can lead to impairment of the voice function.

Nicotine and alcohol alter the supply of blood to the mucous membrane in the larynx. This affects the condition of the mucous membrane and the consistency of the mucus. The vibration capacity and the roll off of the mucous membrane described above are restricted or even cancelled out. In order to compensate for this, more pressure is automatically employed. Clarity of vocal sound is lost and the voice begins to sound husky, rough, choked and hoarse. Passive smoking coupled with speaking loudly, for example, in a pub with a high level of noise, can also lead to an impairment of vocal production.

Unfortunately, when vocal problems first arise they are often exacerbated by inappropriate action. The action of coughing in an attempt to get rid of phlegm and clear the voice only results in putting strain on the vocal folds. Nobody would think of trying to get rid of dirt from a polished surface by using sandpaper.

The belief that whispering will give your voice a chance to recover is also a misconception. The act of whispering actually puts more strain on the vocal cords than does the act of speaking in a normal voice. In order truly to preserve the voice it needs proper rest. It is very difficult to adhere to this, as it goes against people's normal need to communicate, but it is the best way of relieving a 'scratched' larynx.

Sound is Created from a Tone

Resonance in the Vocal Tract

The region above the glottis, which is also called the vocal tract, is where the voice is 'formed'. The vocal tract serves as the resonance area and forms vocal sound from the primary laryngeal tone. The condition of the vocal tract is responsible for variation in timbre, that is, the position of the tongue, how wide open the lower jaw is, the amount of tension and the position of the lips, tension in the cheeks, tongue, soft palate and all the muscles in the mouth and neck region.

The position of the larynx is decisive in determining the size of the vocal tract. When the diaphragm sinks the larynx also sinks so that the vocal tract becomes enlarged at the lower end. In the case of excessive tension the larynx is pulled upwards and the resonance area is diminished.

Changes to the vocal tract give rise to vocal sounds being formed into different vowels. Hence vowels (a, e, i, and so on) are not formed in the larynx but in the mouth region. The size and width of the vocal tract directly influence the clarity, sound and capacity of the vowels (Figure 5.4).

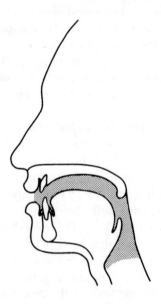

Figure 5.4: Illustration of the vocal tract

A grand piano differs from a standard piano primarily on account of its having a much larger resonance space. For concerts the lid of a grand piano is opened so that the resonance space is further increased and its capacity thereby augmented.

Upper Partials

When we clink glasses at a social occasion we can tell whether the glasses are made of valuable crystal or simply of pressed glass. When we tap against a bowl we can also tell whether it is made of porcelain or pottery and we can even tell by the sound it makes whether the bowl is undamaged or has a flaw. So we are familiar with the idea of sound as a 'sign of quality'.

We can tell one instrument from another and can hear whether a wood or a brass instrument is being played. Every violin resonates slightly differently from any other violin. Stringed instruments resonate in a different way to wind instruments, and people also sound different, despite the fact that they may be singing the same tone.

There is a physical basis for this phenomenon: the upper partials. Upper partials are resonating frequencies in a frequency area of a manifold (basic) tone. If two instruments play the same note, different frequencies are stimulated to resonate in the area of the upper partials.

Every (basic) tone has a countless number of upper partials, and the upper partial areas of particular intensity are called formants. In human voices the formants are decisive for vowel differentiation, tonal timbre and the capacity of a voice.

We are familiar with the effect of formants when using the telephone. The telephone is particularly good at transmitting this frequency area of upper partials of our voices, so that we can easily recognise people by their characteristic vocal features.

Tonal Colour (Timbre)

The structure of the formants in the vocal tract is what determines whether the voice sounds tight, strangled, full, round, sharp, metallic, soft, and so on. These terms describe tonal colour, also called 'timbre'.

Differences in tonal colour are a result of different vibrational activity of the individual sound 'bodies'. No other term would better express the significance of the body for voice production. This is what indicates that our whole body is involved in the resonance process. The direct resonance of the vocal tract is therefore complemented by the body's resonance.

6
Articulation

In the previous chapter we explained how tone is formed in the vocal tract and how this leads to the formation of vowels. This is why it is called the vocal tract.

All consonants are also formed in the vocal tract. Articulatory activity and vocal sound are closely linked. If somebody cannot 'open their mouth' this will disadvantageously affect the intelligibility of their articulation as well as the vocal sound.

Articulatory Organs

The term 'articulatory organs' is in actual fact incorrect, because 'organs' is not used in the usual sense of the word. One also speaks of articulators, which include upper and lower lip, both rows of teeth, the alveolars, the hard palate, the soft palate and the tongue (Figure 6.1).

Formation of Speech Sounds

If air flows, for example, between a narrow passage that is formed between the upper incisors and the bottom lip, then the sound 'f' is produced. If a tone is simultaneously formed in the larynx a 'w' sound is produced. All sounds are produced in the mouth region through movement and different positions of the articulatory organs.

The soft palate rises when forming speech sounds and rests against the back wall of the throat. This causes the air-tone stream to be oral, that is, to pass through the mouth. The nasal sounds 'n', 'm' and 'ng' are an exception. When these sounds are formed, as is also the case with nasal vowels in French, the soft palate does not form a blockage against the back wall of the throat and the air completely or partly flows through the nose.

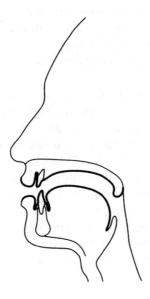

Figure 6.1: Illustration of the articulatory organs

For the formation of the described vowels a certain amount of tensing of the muscles involved in the articulation process is necessary. The correct measure of articulatory tension and the physiological speech movements that arise thereof are closely linked to the interaction with the tension of the laryngeal muscles, that is, to vocal production.

Articulation as a Means of Expression

On a personal level, clear articulation is equated with resoluteness.

We are familiar with the words 'to express oneself' in our use of language. What we mean by this is to make oneself understood. The very way and means by which somebody articulates him- or herself alters, irrespective of the content, the force of what is said. If, for example, someone tries to defend him- or herself in an argument and his or her articulation is 'feeble', that person will be less convincing. A certain will to form and shape words is required for clear articulation. It is necessary to 'set about' the (speech) sounds. Fröschels (1940) clearly demonstrated the functional relationship of biting or chewing and speaking and developed the 'chewing method' for voice therapy. That biting and chewing are of very personal importance is demonstrated by Perls. In his book *Das Ich, der Hunger und die Aggression* ['The Self, Hunger and Aggression'] (1987) he describes how biting off and subsequently breaking down with teeth are actions that are simultaneously aggressive and vital (compare Chapter 9, Exercise 32).

The articulatory organs, mouth, lower jaw and lips can say a lot about the condition a person is in. We are familiar with children's mouths standing agape when they are astounded or of being advised to bite our lip when faced with a difficult situation.

We associate a downturned mouth with sadness, disappointment or ill-humour. We also know what the pouting lips that accompany offence look like and, finally, our lips form to kiss when we want to express our affection for someone.

In our language usage there are expressions that seemingly just describe articulation, but in actual fact say something more, for example, 'to speak with a forked tongue' or 'to have a loose tongue'.

7
Tonus and Intention

A certain tension of the muscles is necessary for all movements of the body. As breathing and voice production are also movements, their activity is directly influenced by and dependent on body tension (tonus). The regulation of body tension occurs via the gamma nervous system.

The body tension of a person may be too low, too high, or 'just right' with respect to the situation in question. We also talk of slackness, exertion/strain, tenseness.

Body Tension and Intention

In order to find or create the right tension what is required is the mental power to imagine, the openness or adjustment to a situation. The term 'intention' (Coblenzer and Muhar, 1976) has become firmly ingrained in voice therapy for this.

For example, in the case of tension adjustment by intention:

We are familiar with the phenomenon of walking on the stairs in the dark and of not coming across a step that we presumed was there, we 'tap' into thin air, in doing this, we have taken the last step using incorrect muscle tension.

If we step on to a frozen lake in winter we do this with great caution to test whether the sheet of ice is thick enough. It would not be hard to imagine that the same sheet of ice would break if we were to make a clumsy movement, despite no difference in body weight.

Similarly, the one and same child seems light when carried because it wants to see something, and heavier when it is asleep.

Our objective, our intention, clearly alters our muscle tension. This 'mechanism' normally functions in the case of speaking or voice production. The intention to speak causes optimal tensing of all muscles involved in the act of speaking and manifests itself in mime and gesticulation.

There are several ways in which the co-operation of intention and muscle tension may be disturbed:

1. The state of tension of individual muscles, groups of muscles or the entire body muscles are fixed. This means it is no longer possible to alter the tonus with a respective intention since body tension is permanently too strong or too weak.
2. A person's intention is either unclear, hardly existent or non-existent. The muscles do not even 'know' which tension they need to build up.
3. The intention is exaggerated and too much tension is built up for the situation at hand.

Accordingly, as far as therapy is concerned the main aim of voice therapy in the field of tonus is to bring about awareness of body tension as a whole or in part (compare Chapter 2, pp. 20–25), in order to realise how body tension can change and to learn how it can be regulated.

Body Tension and Posture

Body tension is also expressed in posture, which has important implications for voice function. A sunken chest will hinder the physiological breathing function because the diaphragm is prevented from expanding to the full at the bottom, meaning that the lungs can only fully expand in the upper part of the thorax. If the head is bent forward this causes a kink in the vocal tract and prevents it from being used to its full capacity as a resonance space. These descriptions concern the functional meaning of posture.

It should, however, be kept in mind that the exterior posture of a person often reflects his or her inner state: pride causes the chest to swell, the head is bowed in humility, suffering doubles up a body.

We speak of light-footedness or stubbornness, and thereby refer to the characteristics of a person.

The consequences that these 'embodiments' of feelings and modes of conduct have for work on the voice are that strengthening posture and work on the body should not simply be functional but should always occur in conjunction with personal aspects.

Part III
Exercises

8
Introduction to Exercises

The following series of exercises has been devised for two different target groups: for those practising voice development therapy and for voice therapists.

For those practising voice development therapy the exercises offer the possibility of working under their own direction. The limits of such independent work, however, lie in the fact that speaking is a communicative activity, which means that conversation partners are a necessity. In particular, the exercises in the second half of the exercise collection, designed to train intentional partner-oriented speech, will be restricted.

Moreover, learning the exercises is much easier under the instruction of trained therapists.

This means that the collection of exercises is most effective if used as a complementary or independent continuation of therapeutic work.

For therapists, the collection of exercises is meant as an instrument in the use of PVT. We turn to questions on therapy that arise in conjunction in Part IV of the book. For therapeutic work with the collection of exercises, one's own experience of the exercises is of vital importance.

Sources of the Exercises

In the course of the last centuries numerous methods and exercises from the most diverse disciplines have been integrated into work on the voice. It is not always possible to trace the origins of the individual exercises. They have been modified by various therapists for work on the voice in accordance with main points of concern and personal experiences. We must therefore confine ourselves to referring to very general therapeutic concepts, teachings or voice-pedagogic directions that have also become the basis of our work on the voice. Essentially these are:

Eutonie, Gerda Alexander
Feldenkrais method
Alexander technique
Breathing work, Ilse Middendorf
Breathing therapy, Elena Cardas
Breathing meditation, Hetty Draayer
Breathing and voice work, Coblenzer
Voice therapy, Ruth Dinkelacker
Voice therapy, Almuth Eberle.

PVT always takes bodily self-awareness into consideration in its exercises and goes on the assumption that it is possible to learn through self-regulation.

In principle, PVT gets by with very few exercises. It is not a question of continually trying something new, but of repeatedly having new experiences using the same exercises.

Division of the Collection of Exercises

The collection of exercises is divided into four areas: tonus, breathing, phonation and articulation. There is a further sub-division of these areas into sections or partial objectives. Exercises 1–37 focus on achieving basic physiological voice function. This often makes further work on the subsequent section obsolete, so exercises 38–47 only serve to flesh out the work on specific functions.

Each exercise is devised as an individual unit consisting of three parts:

1. description of the exercise
2. functional level
3. personal level.

We see it as important that an exercise is not carried out from a purely functional aspect, in isolation. Each individual exercise is designed to be intelligible with regard to meaning, content and significance for the individual. This is why the functional and personal level of the exercise is considered subsequent to the description of the exercise. We have had to accept repetitions in the text, which arise by force:

- for contextual reasons, in order to maintain the structure or unity;
- for formal reasons, in order to avoid the reader's having to turn back to previous pages.

Although each individual exercise is a unit in itself, all the exercises are built up on one another in accordance with the structure of vocal function. This means that it is necessary for you to familiarise yourself with the entire collection of exercises. Having gained further experience in conducting the exercises, individual programmes should evolve for those practising voice development. A description of the content of the individual units of each exercise follows.

Description of the Exercises

The exercises have been formulated in such a way as to make them as intelligible as possible, enabling them to be used for independent work. Once you get to know the exercises it should be possible for you to orient yourself by referring to the cue in the left-hand margin.

If the exercises are formulated in full, inexperienced therapists might be tempted to read off the exercise instructions. This would defeat the whole object of our work. Justice can only be done to taking a personal approach if the therapists come up with their own formulations, taking the individuality and the personal pace of the clients into consideration. This is why we also reject pre-recorded tapes. If the client so wishes, we do allow this in the case of their personal treatment, body and breathing exercises (not in the case of voice exercises) so they have an initial aid with which to practise at home.

The Functional Level

The basis for gaining an understanding of the functional level of the exercises is presented in Part II of the book. On the basis of this, each individual exercise has cues which clearly denote which function is being worked on in each exercise.

The Personal Level

A concrete contextual description of the personal level of an exercise is not possible.

What actuates an exercise on a personal level is as diverse as people are diverse. To expect a specific effect on the part of the practising person as well as the therapists would be a functionalisation of the personal level. Our annotations are therefore to be considered as thought-provokers that are meant to encourage reflection after the exercise.

Furthermore, explanations for a better understanding of the exercises are to be found under this heading.

9
Collection of Exercises

Tonus

EXERCISE 1: Lying down

Lying on your back	Lie on your back on the floor. Arms resting at your sides. Legs lying as wide apart as your hips. Feet turned outwards resting in a relaxed position. Eyes closed. To relax your neck muscles you may choose to rest your head on a firm support (for example, a thick phone book).
Sensing contact surface	Now sense the contact surface of your body. Start with the right foot and sense where it touches the ground and where there is a distance from the ground. Go through the whole body in the following order: right leg – left leg; right arm – left arm; trunk; head; entire body.
Loosen lower jaw	Relax your lower jaw. Lips resting gently together so that your mouth is still closed. Feel how much space there is in the cavity of your mouth. Always make sure that your lower jaw is relaxed when performing all exercises.
Finishing exercise	Stretch your limbs close to your body. The movements should be done slowly. Lie on your side and draw up your legs. Assume a sitting position by propping yourself up on your arms. Your head should be raised last of all. Reaching a sitting a position in this way takes the pressure off the neck region.

Functional level:
Achieving eutonus through proprioception.
Reduction or building-up of tension depending on the state of tension when the exercise is commenced. Relax your lower jaw: creates space in the cavity of your mouth, in preparation for yawning wide.

Assume sitting position: training use of body, relieving neck muscles.
Finish exercise slowly: relieves circulation.

Personal level:
This is the exercise with which person-oriented work on the voice
usually starts. This can be a giant leap of a first step.
Lying on the ground doing nothing makes us confront ourselves.
When we do this we relinquish our habitual professional or familiar
role and 'only remain' human beings.
This may trigger off nervousness and even fear.
But it is also possible to experience positive reactions. We can enjoy
the feeling of not having to do anything and of being carried by the
ground.
In both cases the exercise has the effect of making us get in touch
with ourselves.

EXERCISE 2: Comparing tonus

Lying on your back	Lie on your back on the floor. Arms resting at your sides. Legs lying as wide apart as your hips. Feet turned outwards resting in a relaxed position. Eyes closed. To relax your neck muscles you may choose to rest your head on a firm support (for example, a thick phone book).
Sensing the contact surface	Sense the contact surface of both legs simultaneously. Where is there distance from the ground? From the legs move on to your arms, trunk and finally to your head. If you lose concentration, refocus your thoughts on whichever part of your body you want to concentrate on, without letting yourself get annoyed.
Space in the cavity of your mouth	Make sure that your jaw is not tensed and sense the space in the cavity of your mouth.
Comparing tonus	Move your right leg slowly and while doing so sense any changes in the contact surface. Experiment with the movements you can make, but ensure that your leg always remains in contact with the floor. Afterwards put your leg back in the starting position and compare it to your left leg. What differences do you sense? Do the same thing with the left leg and then compare both legs again.
Finishing exercise	Stretch your limbs close to your body. Pay attention to your movements. Lie on your side and draw up your legs. Assume a sitting position by propping yourself up on your arms. Your head should be raised last of all.

Functional level:
By means of comparison you are able to perceive tonus.
Teaching body awareness.
Tonus can be influenced (gamma motoricity).

Personal level:
Slow 'unathletic' movement of the body is something new to many people. People often feel 'funny' and their movements are unsure. Our general mode of conduct is expressed in the way that we carry out movements. Movements may, for example, be over-hasty, undue or hesitant and not flowing. To perceive and reflect on this may provide us with a different understanding of ourselves and our behaviour, and can create a link to our voice problems. Trying out different movements and enjoying improvising gives us the chance to widen our playing field.

Sufficient time should always be set aside for comparing each worked-on side with the other, regardless of the fact that you may already be familiar with an exercise and its effect. This is how you are repeatedly trained to become aware of a current situation, that is, of being 'here and now'. Our reactions to an exercise may be very similar, but time and again differences arise.

Being conscious of these differences leads to a change in body awareness and contact with oneself.

EXERCISE 3: Sitting

Sitting on chair

Sit upright on a chair. You can lean against the back of the chair, but your back should be straight. Legs as wide apart as your hips, knees a little lower than pelvis. Feet resting parallel on the ground. Eyes closed.
If the chair measurements are not correct for your body size, create a balance either by raising the seat (if you have long legs) or by placing a firm support (for example, a phone book) beneath your feet (in the case of short legs).
Hands resting relaxed on thighs.

Perceive contact area

Perceive contact areas in the following order:
– Feet in relation to the ground: which parts are closer to the ground, which further away from it? How big are your feet?
– Thighs and buttocks on the chair: where does the contact start?
– How large is the surface that has contact with the seat of the chair?
– Back against the back of the chair: Where does your back touch?
– Hands on thighs: where are your hands placed? Are your fingers straight or bent? Are your hands touching each other?

Perceiving the body as a whole

Now become aware of all points of contact simultaneously.
How do you feel in relation to the ground and chair?
What feelings do you experience?
Has the exercise altered your frame of mind?

Functional level:
Regulating of tonus.
Preparation for your sitting position, which is a necessary condition for deep breathing and the development of resonance.

Personal level:
Being conscious of yourself whilst sitting still is a simple exercise which is very effective. It enables you to experience inner calm and composure and get in touch with yourself. The influence on soul and mind in addition to bodily well-being becomes evident. Emotional agitation may vanish and allow for more lucid thinking. If initial problems are experienced when performing this exercise it may be because you are not used to 'doing nothing'.

This exercise runs through work on the voice and will later be combined with centring and calm breathing. All exercises that are carried out in a sitting position start with this procedure.

EXERCISE 4: Standing
You will need a tennis ball for this exercise.

Roll the tennis ball Place a tennis ball underneath your foot whilst in a standing position and roll it back and forth on the ground, massaging the sole of your foot.

Stand on the tennis ball Now place the tennis ball underneath your right heel and continue standing on it. Sense how large the area of your foot is that comes into contact with the ball. After a while stand on the ball with the arch of your metatarsus and then on the ball of your foot. Finally 'grip' the ball with your toes making sure they do not tense up.

Redirecting pain If you experience pain in your foot while conducting this exercise, balance the tension by shifting your weight on to your other foot. Also imagine your foot is going through the ball and making contact with the floor and any pain is being redirected into the ground. It is important that no other part of your body becomes tense.

Compare Stand with both feet on the ground and compare your feet.
Do you feel a difference?
What does the size of your right foot feel like in comparison to your left foot?
Does contact in relation to the floor differ?
Now run through the exercise with your left foot and again compare both your sides.

Functional level:
Stimulation of the reflex zones causes an increase of the tonus.
Working through of the whole body (enlivens).
Preparation for your standing position.

Personal level:
By comparing both feet in this exercise, differences in tonus can easily be felt. This also applies to people practising voice develop-

ment who still have very little experience in the practice of bodily self-perception. A number of people are also impressed by the effect it has on their temperament. It is not only the body that feels refreshed, since general mood improves and it becomes easier to think. This exercise is a good substitute for coffee and can enable one to make an easier start to the day.

A good relation of the feet to the ground, 'being rooted' is a necessary condition for upright posture when standing. All work with feet prepares you for this.

EXERCISE 5: Massaging the feet

Stroking the foot   Sit on a chair without armrests and place your
                           right foot on your left thigh.
                           Stroke your foot with light and gentle
                           movements imagining that you want to do
                           something good for your foot.

Massaging the heel Start massaging the area of your foot above
                           the heel. Clasp your heel by placing your
                           thumb on one side and your index and ring
                           finger on the other. Massage these points by
                           making small circular movements with your
                           fingers (pressure point massage) until you
                           have worked through the whole area above
                           the heel.

Massaging the arch Now massage the arch of your foot with your
of the foot   two thumbs in the same way.
                           Use sufficient pressure to alleviate tension in
                           the foot, but make sure that it always feels
                           agreeable.
                           Make sure that your shoulder girdle and the
                           cavity of your mouth are in a relaxed state.

Massaging and   Now turn to your toes. Press all around each
moving the toes   individual toe. Afterwards move your toes
                           back and forth with your hands. When you
                           have finished, stroke the whole of your foot
                           with both hands, as above.

Compare   Now place both feet next to each other on the
                           floor and compare them.
                           Is there a difference between the feet, and
                           what is that difference?
                           Has this exercise had an effect on the whole
                           right side of your body?
                           Afterwards massage your left foot in the same
                           way and sense whether you feel a difference
                           again.

Functional level:
Reflex zones, stimulation of the whole body.
Increase of tonus (enlivens).
Improvement of perceptual ability.
Preparation for standing.

Personal level:
Massaging your own body means focusing on yourself. We often do not take the time to do this. This is especially true of the feet. They are not as important to us as, for example, our face, despite the fact that our well-being and mobility are very dependent on our feet.

The stimulating effect of this exercise may serve as a substitute for stimulants such as coffee, tea, and so on.

EXERCISE 6: Shifting pressure using the ground

Lying down	Lie on your back on the floor. Arms resting at your sides with your hands resting on their sides. Legs lying as wide apart as your hips. Feet turned outwards resting in a relaxed position. Eyes closed.

Stationing your legs Imagine that there is a puppet string attached to your right knee. By means of this thread your knee is raised in the direction of the ceiling so that eventually the sole of your foot is standing squarely on the ground.
Let your left leg rise in the same way (do the same with your left leg). Both legs are next to each other placed as wide apart as your hips, feet as close as possible to your buttocks.

Pressing flatly across the floor Imagine that you are wearing skis on your feet and want to glide flatly across the floor. However, your feet remain where they are so that you are only exerting pressure in this direction and letting go.
The rest of your body should be passive. Observe how it reacts to the shifting of pressure. Is the impulse generated in the soles of your feet transmitted or are there blockages in the body that prevent this from happening?
Experiment with shifting pressure by trying out slow and fast movements. Savour the impulse surging through your body.

Pressing against the wall A variant is to exert pressure against a wall. Lie in front of a wall, raising your legs so that your feet are placed against the wall and your legs form a right angle. Now press hard against the wall with your feet, imagining that you are trying to push the wall away. Again, the rest of the body should be passive, but should react to the shifting of pressure.

Lying down   At the end of the exercise remain in a lying position for a moment, with your legs stretched out, and perceive what the contact surface of your back is like.

Functional level:
Stimulation and strengthening of the atrophied spinal muscles in the case of bad posture, for example, lordosis.
Simultaneously has an effect on the inner back muscles.
Significance of spinal column for posture. Has repercussions for the voice production area.

Personal level:
This exercise is often not easy. Although we are 'doing' something (exerting pressure) we are supposed to 'let be' (the rest of the body). In this exercise the blockages can clearly be sensed in our body. If we are able to clear these we will be more permeable and will be able to feel the regenerating effect of this exercise.

EXERCISE 7: Pressing into the ground

Lying down

Lie on your back on the floor. Arms resting at your sides with your hands resting on their edges.
Legs lying as wide apart as your hips.
Feet turned outwards resting in a relaxed position.
Eyes closed.

Stationing your legs

Imagine that there is a puppet string attached to your right knee. By means of this thread your knee is raised in the direction of the ceiling so that eventually the sole of your foot is standing squarely on the ground.
Let your left leg rise in the same way (do the same with your left leg). Both legs are placed as wide apart as your hips next to each other, feet as close as possible to your buttocks.

Pressing into the ground

Press into the ground with the soles of your feet. Observe how your pelvis eventually rises from the ground. Your abdomen should remain relaxed and you should be breathing calmly and regularly. To verify that this is the case, place one hand on your abdominal wall. Only let your spine rise as far from the ground as happens of its own accord from the pressure of your feet.
Then let your spine slowly sink back to the ground. Perceive how the vertebrae roll off one another.

Finishing exercise

Sense how you feel for a moment and stretch afterwards. Slowly assume a sitting position.

Functional level:
Stimulation and strengthening of the atrophied spinal muscles in the case of bad posture, for example, damage to posture or hollow back.
Simultaneously has an effect on the inner back muscles.

Significance of spinal column for posture. Has repercussions for the vocal production area.

Personal level:
With this exercise, as in Exercise 6, permeability is experienced. Sometimes it is not possible to relax the spinal column without jerky movements. It becomes clear where we support ourselves. It is often the pelvic region that is stiff and intercepts the energy streaming from this area.

EXERCISE 8: Sitting

Perceive sitting position	Remain for a moment in the position that you have just assumed. Perceive: are your legs next to each other or crossed? Is your back straight or hunched? Is your abdominal and chest region restricted or free for breathing? Is the back of your neck bent? What is the position of the larynx?
Experimenting with straightening your neck	Lean your head as far back as possible into the nape of your neck and move it slowly from a backward to a forward position, until your chin is close to your collarbone. If you make an 'oh' sound at the same time as you make the movement, does the sound change along with your altered head position? When is it emitted most freely? Can you recall the position you were previously in? What is the position of your larynx?
Evening out chair measurements	Sit on the front third of a chair that has a flat seat. Your knees should on no account be higher than your hip joints. If necessary even out the measurements of the chair. If your legs are too short place a firm support (for example, a thick phone book) underneath your feet. If your legs are too long, sit on the support.
Establishing sitting position	Place your hands beneath your buttocks for a moment so that you can feel your ischia. Now exert pressure on the seat of the chair with your ischia (press your ischia down) so that your back slowly straightens up. Hands lying on thighs. Shoulders spread wide, but drooping downwards. A useful image for the picture is a coat-hanger which has bent-down ends.

Shifting the centre of gravity   In this upright position experiment with shifting the centre of gravity. Shift it slightly in front of your ischia then on to it and then slightly to the back of it. When does your back feel it is supporting itself most easily of its own accord?

Sitting calmly   For any activities done in a sitting position it is preferable to sit up straight without leaning against anything. In order to sit calmly use the whole of the seat and put your back right up against the back of the chair. However, only rest the lower part of your back against the back of the chair, so that the centre of gravity remains in the pelvis.

Relaxing the back   Having experimented with this perhaps unfamiliar physiological posture, let your back relax. Sit sideways on a chair, place your hands around one knee and draw it towards you. By doing this your back curves. In this posture rock back and forth on the chair.

Functional level:
Strengthening of the possibly atrophied back muscles. Effect of posture on breathing and resonance. Significance of head posture for intonation through changing of vocal tract. Affects alertness and the ability to concentrate.

Personal level:
We use the term 'posture' with reference to bodily/physical as well as psychological-spiritual conduct. It is easy to find out how both are connected. Sitting up straight can give us the feeling of calmness, security, presence and sovereignty. This does not mean that we are supposed to feign an outward state which we are not in. Altering of the way we sit is a fundamental change because it concerns our entire conduct. Initially it may give rise to negative feelings (for example, to that of being too dominant). It is only possible to grow into the 'correct' posture slowly. Everyday life is the practice field.

EXERCISE 9: Standing

Sliding across the floor with the feet
Sit upright on the front third of the chair. Perceive the connection between chair and floor.

Imagine that your right foot is gliding along the floor as if being pulled by a thread. When doing so, be conscious of the material that your foot is gliding over (for example, carpet). Then choose a different surface (for example, a blanket) and sense what it now feels like.

Compare
Place both feet next to each other and compare them. Is there a difference between the feet in terms of contact area, weight, size, temperature, and so on?

Afterwards do the same with the left foot and compare again.

Porous knees
Now stand up firmly on both feet. Perceive what the connection of your feet to the ground is like.

Now turn your attention to your knees. Straighten them and then let them relax. Perceive the effect that this movement has for the shape and position of your spinal column. At the end remain standing with straight, but loose, porous knees.

Straightened-up pelvis
Place both hands on your hips and tip your pelvis back and forth.

Also experiment with this exercise.

At the end remain standing with your pelvis straightened up.

Drooping shoulders
Let your arms hang by the sides of your body and your shoulders droop. It may be helpful to imagine that you have weights attached to the tips of your fingers.

Sense whether your shoulders are wide open.

It may help if you imagine the three open wings of an altar.

The head is held erect as an extension of the spinal column.

Functional level:

Significance of upright posture for breathing and larynx.

Raising of tonus when standing. Especially important for speakers, singers and players of wind instruments.

Personal level:

Human beings have upright bodies and therefore have possibilities that animals do not. Our language indicates that an upright posture is not necessarily only a bodily event, for example, 'to stand by someone'. We have a 'standpoint' that we can best represent if we are present in our full size. This can have an immediate effect on our self-confidence. Many people's posture is incorrect and they do not feel comfortable when they are coached into a physiological posture for the first time. They might feel too tall or too dominant. As is the case with sitting posture, this change of conduct takes getting used to and must be accompanied by the desire 'to be present in the world' in a different way.

EXERCISE 10: Walking

Standing	Stand on both feet, legs as wide apart as your hips. Run each foot across the floor several times, so that you become aware of the soles of your feet.

Then stand on both feet again and concentrate on three points in the soles of your feet: the ball of the large toe, ball of the little toe and heel.

Remain rooted in this way for a while.

Swinging to and fro Perceive the light movement of your body caused by breathing despite your appearing to be standing completely still. Go along with this movement and let it occur unhindered. By doing so you will eventually start swinging back and forth. Find your own rhythm. Ensure that your lower jaw is relaxed and that the entire sole of each foot remains in contact with the ground.

To finish this exercise come to a standstill and sense what you feel.

Has the swinging brought about a different frame of mind in you?

Walking Shift your weight forwards, start walking by freeing one foot from the ground.

With every step you take exert a little resistance towards the ground. Let your feet joints move in a supple manner.

Ways of walking compared Remain standing still and assume a slouched posture. Start walking in this posture and perceive how you feel in the process.

Afterwards stand still, assume a straight posture and start walking in the same way as described above. Be conscious of how your feet leave and touch the ground again. Can you tell the difference?

Functional level:
Improvement of proprioception.
Standing up straight and creation of balance.
Muscular interplay, entire tonus.

Personal level:
Swinging movements can be calming. Think of the swinging to and fro or rocking of a child. Bodily balance is a necessary condition of being able to swing in the first place, and leads to psychological balance. The times you have to wait standing (waiting for a bus, in queues or at a shop counter) can be used as practice times. The movement can either be done so subtly that it is outwardly imperceptible or just imagined.

All walking that is necessary during the course of the day can also be turned into an exercise. Often conscious upright walking has a positive effect on our mood. Furthermore we 'tread more assuredly' if our footsteps are firm.

If our feet consciously show resistance to the ground we may find it easier to deal with confrontation.

EXERCISE 11: Sensitising the sacrum

Lying down

Lie on your back on the floor. Arms resting at your sides with your hands resting on their edges.
Legs lying as wide apart as your hips.
Feet turned outwards resting in a relaxed position.
Eyes closed.

Raising legs

Let your legs rise, imagining that they are being pulled up by a thread, so that both soles of your feet are next to each other on the ground.

Shifting the centre of gravity vertically

Imagine that you have the face of a clock on the back of your pelvis. Now shift the centre of gravity of the contact area from digit 6 (coccyx) to digit 12 (5th lumbar vertebra). Repeat this small movement several times slowly and with ease.

Shifting the centre of gravity horizontally

Now shift your pelvis from one side to the other (from digit 3 to 9). Your legs may react in a different way. Your knees may go back and forth like a windscreen wiper or they may stay in one place. Experiment with both possibilities.

Circling

Circling the clock, now shift your weight from one imaginary digit to another. Try doing this in a clockwise and then anti-clockwise direction. In this way encircle your sacrum. Make sure that the movements are not large ones. Ensure they are done slowly and smoothly.

Perceiving the contact area

One after the other, let your legs glide slowly to the ground so that you are lying with your legs stretched out. Sense how your pelvis lies on the ground.

End the exercise by stretching and assume a sitting position via your side.

Functional level:
Sensitisation of the sacrum, straightening-up reflex.
Significance of spinal column for posture, diaphragmatic suspension, straightening-out of the larynx
Deep centring of gravity, yawning tension in the midriff.

Personal level:
Working in the abdominal-pelvic region means that we turn our attention to a part of our body which is really a taboo area. This is an intimate area where the excretory and sexual organs are located. At the same time this part of our body is the area of our vital energy and a source of energy that is all too often underused.

EXERCISE 12: Rotating the pelvis

Lying down

Lie on your back on the floor. Arms resting at your sides with your hands resting on their edges.
Legs lying as wide apart as your hips.
Feet turned outwards resting in a relaxed position.
Eyes closed.
Perceive what the contact area of your pelvis is like.

Knees over chest

Put your legs up and imagine the traction power in your knees. Now imagine that your knees are being drawn up, until they reach your chest.
Place one foot on top of the other, so that your feet are crossed.
What does the contact area of your pelvis feel like in this position?

Bending the arms

Bending your arms, rest them next to your head, like babies often do.

Rocking the knees

Guide your closed legs slowly first to the right and then to the left. Only go as far in the direction of the floor as you can without removing your shoulders from the ground.
With gentle movements rock back and forth for a while.
Pay attention to space in the cavity of your mouth and to breathing calmly.
Then let your legs glide to the ground and rest for a moment.

Rotating the pelvis

Let your knees rise again. With your legs closed draw a circle in the air, allowing your pelvis to rotate.
Make sure your movements are gentle and smooth and that you do not hold your breath.

Perceiving contact surfaces   Let your legs glide to the ground and lie down stretched out flat on your back. To begin with perceive the contact surface of your pelvis and then your entire body.

End the exercise by stretching and slowly assume a sitting position via your side.

Functional level:

Significance of spinal column for posture, diaphragmatic suspension, straightening-out of the larynx.

Emphasis in the depth, yawning tension in the belt area.

Personal level:

Like Exercise 11, this exercise is aimed at vitality in the abdominal-pelvic region. It is important that the movements are not done mechanically, but that all changes and blockages that may exist are perceived and accepted.

The sensing of an enlarged abdominal-pelvic area may at first be experienced as something unpleasant since it does not correspond with the generally prevalent ideal of slimness.

EXERCISE 13: Centring

Sitting	Sit up straight on the front third of a chair. Your legs as wide apart as your hips. Place your feet parallel on the ground. Eyes closed.
Rooting the feet	Imagine that roots are growing from your feet into the ground. One root is growing from the ball of your big toe, another from the ball of your little toe and a third from your heel. Imagine that the roots are growing deep into the ground.
Rooting the pelvis	Now, without losing the roots in your feet, let three roots grow from your pelvic floor. Two roots from your ischia, the third from the extension of your spine.
Triangles in the soles of your feet	Go back to the soles of your feet and imagine linking the three root points so that they form a triangle. The triangle is an aperture through which you can let all the tension in your body, your feelings and thoughts flow into the ground. Enjoy the feeling of becoming completely empty.
Triangles in the pelvic floor	Imagine that your two ischia and extended coccyx are linked by lines, so that a triangle is formed on your pelvic floor. Here again let your tension drain from it.
Think of a bowl	Focus on your middle, which is located beneath your navel and is the width of a hand. Place your hands on your lower stomach in such a way that the tips of your fingers touch each other at this point. After a while make a mental link to the sacrum which lies opposite. In order to do this place the back of a hand on the sacrum. Imagine a connecting line that runs from one hand to the other through your body.

Then link these two points by imagining a line that runs round your body: from the front around one side to the sacrum and from there round the other side back to the front again. This line forms the upper rim of a bowl that extends to the pelvic floor. Imagine that you are sitting in this bowl.

Finishing exercise   Place your hands on your thighs and sense how you are sitting on the chair. What frame of mind has this exercise put you in? How do you feel physically and mentally? Slowly open your eyes by blinking several times.
End the exercise by stretching slowly.

Functional level:
Regulation of tonus.
Emphasis in the depth, precondition for unimpeded movement of diaphragm.

Personal level:
The significance of centring was described in detail in Chapter 2, pp. 23–25. But it is only your own experience of working on your middle that makes you aware of the full meaning of centring. Reactions are as varied as people. The important thing is that we let all our feelings happen, that we do not just expect positive reactions. To centre yourself means to put yourself at the centre of attention and to perceive 'what is', without forming a judgement.

EXERCISE 14: Lying down

Lying down	Lie on your back on the floor. Arms resting at your sides with your hands resting on their edges. Legs lying as wide apart as your hips. Feet turned outwards resting in a relaxed position. Eyes closed.
Awareness of the pelvis	Before the upper part of the body can be worked on it is necessary to centre yourself in the pelvis. Let your knees rise so that they are above the abdomen-chest area. Experiment with the contact surface of your pelvis by making circular movements. Then let your legs gently glide to the floor one after another so that you are lying stretched out on your back again.
Arm movement	Imagine the following movement before actually doing it. Let your extended right arm rise drawing a wide backward arc, so that it finally comes to rest next to your head. Leave your arm in this position for a while and sense the passive stretching in the shoulder area. Then, drawing a wide arc through the air, let your arm return. Repeat this movement several times and observe how the contact area of your shoulders keeps changing. Then compare both sides and repeat the same movement with your left arm.
Head movement	Turn your head to the left, so that your ear touches or almost touches the ground. The end of your nose guides your movement so that your head instantly turns. Leave your mouth slightly open during this process. Sense how this causes the right side of your nape and the neck muscles to stretch

passively. Let your head remain in this position for a while and then slowly return to the starting position. Repeat this movement several times. Compare both sides before you turn your head to the right.

To end remain in the starting position for a while. Let your concentration wander through your entire body. Then end the exercise by stretching.

Functional level:
Loosening of shoulder girdle and the outer neck muscles.
Releasing of tension in articulation and phonation area.
De-centring of focus in upper part of body.

Personal level:
There are deep instinctive reasons lying behind tensions in the area of the larynx. This is the point of the body where, by squeezing the windpipe, we can most easily be killed. We instinctively want to protect this point when faced with danger by pulling up our shoulders and lowering our chin. In every instance of fear, even if somebody only wants to 'get at our throat' in the figurative sense, this protective mechanism is triggered. In the long run this causes tensed and aching shoulders. It is only when we have familiarised ourselves with our pelvis that we are capable of letting go of the tension in the upper part of our body and confronting difficult situations with strength drawn from deep within.

EXERCISE 15: Sitting

Sitting	Sit on the front third of a chair. Feet parallel next to each other on the ground. Back straight. Hands resting on thighs.
Perceiving contact area	Perceive the contact points of your body with the ground and chair in the following order: feet; thighs – buttocks; hands (contact with thighs).
Centring in the pelvis	Experiment with the contact area of your buttocks. Shift the weight from one ischium to the other and then in front of and behind the ischia. Then start circling. Relax and sense what you feel.
Shoulder movement	Imagine that you have a paintbrush on your right shoulder. You draw lines in the air with it. Try out the different movements you can make with your shoulder. Your hand should remain on your thigh while doing this. Make sure this movement is done playfully without any kind of effort. Compare both shoulders before you do the movement with the other side.
Head movement	Elongate your head with an imaginary paintbrush and paint lines with it in the air. Make sure that you do not make any rotating movements behind the line of your back. How easily and effortlessly can you perform this movement? Can you keep your neck muscles loose while performing it?

Functional level:
Releasing tension in articulation and phonation area.
Shifting of focal point from above to below.

Personal level:
If tensed muscles are loosened in the shoulder–nape region this sometimes leads to surprising emotions. Diffuse fears or the need to cry may arise. These emotions should not be suppressed but allowed to happen. Most of us have experienced the pain that is felt in the throat caused by trying to hold back tears. Crying can therefore be very constructive and is the expression of consciously experienced feelings or feelings of which we are unconscious.

Many people receive medical treatment because of severe tension in their shoulders and nape. It is possible to gain relief by means of injections or physiotherapy, but in the long run the pain will only disappear when we have trained ourselves in bodily self-perception so that we immediately perceive tension. The aim is to understand why we become tense in particular situations and to learn how we can let go.

EXERCISE 16: Loosening up the shoulders

Sitting	Sit on the front third of a chair. Feet parallel next to each other on the ground. Back straight. Hands resting on thighs.
Perceiving contact area	Perceive the contact points of your body with the ground and chair in the following order: feet; thighs – buttocks hands (contact with thighs).
Centring in the pelvis	Experiment with the contact area of your buttocks. Shift the weight from one ischium to the other and then in front of and behind the ischia. Then start circling. Relax and sense what you feel.
Let your shoulders drop	Pull your shoulders up as far as they will go. Then let them slowly sink again. It may help to picture the sand trickling through an hourglass. Ensure that the movement is smooth and not jerky. Is there a point at which this movement falters? Is it possible for you to sink your shoulders a little further? Repeat this movement several times and take time to sense what you feel before you start to stretch and finish the exercise.

Functional level:
Releasing of tension in articulation and phonation area.
Shifting of focal point from above to below.

Personal level:
This exercise can make us aware of the fact that we continuously have our shoulders raised too high. The point at which the movement falters is usually the point at which the shoulders lock; overcoming this can cause a feeling of relief. 'A weight is lifted from our shoulders.'

EXERCISE 17: With a stick

You will need a small stick made of bamboo (from a garden centre) or wood (for example, chopstick) for this exercise.

Sitting	Sit on the front third of a chair. Legs as wide apart as your hips. Feet parallel to each other on the ground.
Perceiving contact area	Perceive the contact points of your body with the ground and chair in the following order: feet; thighs – buttocks hands (contact with thighs).
Feeling the face and neck	Draw a line with the stick from the middle of your forehead down to your neck, so that you can differentiate between the two sides. Then starting with the right side feel your face in the following order: forehead; eye and cheekbone; half/one side of nose; ear; cheek; half/one side of mouth; chin; neck and nape.
Compare	Now compare how each side felt. What differences can you detect? Feel the left side in the same way and compare again.
Caress face	Then caress your face with both hands from top to bottom letting your lower jaw drop. Try and bring about a gentle yawning through this action. End the exercise by stretching.

Functional level:

Loosening and sensitisation of the face.

Preparation for working on the frontal position of sound.

Improvement of resonance in the vocal tract.

Personal level:

Often the result of extreme mental effort is a tensing up of the face muscles. There is the well known 'thinker's brow' which is not necessarily as a result of thinking. Behind the tension may lie the fear of 'losing face'.

If you stop frowning, cheerfulness often sets in and things become easier to do.

EXERCISE 18: With hands

Sitting	Sit on the front third of a chair. Legs as wide apart as your hips. Feet parallel to each other on the ground.
Perceiving contact area	Perceive the contact points of your body with the ground and chair in the following order: feet; thighs – buttocks; hands (contact with thighs).
Hands on face	Cover your eyes with the balls of your thumbs and clasp your head at the hairline. Concentrate on this contact. Then remove your hands and sense what you feel. Do you now feel more aware of this part of your face? Then clasp your chin with your hands and the sides of your cheeks and be conscious of the contact.
Caress face	Then caress your face with both hands from top to bottom letting your lower jaw drop. Try to bring about a gentle yawning through this action. End the exercise by stretching.

Functional level:
Influence on resonance brought about through the dissolving of tension and the forward projection of the position of sound.

Personal level:
Running your hands across your face or through your hair is often an unconscious gesture you make when things get too much and you feel tense.
But you can also integrate this gesture consciously into everyday life as a means of relaxing and regaining 'clarity'.
The subjects of turning your attention to yourself and treating yourself lovingly may be broached here.

EXERCISE 19: Sinus exercise

Sitting	Sit on the front third of a chair. Legs as wide apart as your hips. Feet parallel to each other on the ground.
Perceiving the contact area	Perceive the contact points of your body with the ground and chair in the following order: feet; thighs – buttocks; hands (contact with thighs).
Massaging the forehead	Place your two index and middle fingers next to each other on the root of your nose. From this point massage your eyebrows and temples by making gentle circular movements with your fingertips while keeping them in one place. Then massage a second horizontal line in the middle of your forehead and finally a third at the end of your forehead.
Massaging cheekbone and nose	Start with pressure point massaging on the inner corner of the eye and then move along the cheekbone to the temple. Then place your thumb and index finger of one hand at the uppermost end of the bridge of the nose and, using pressure point massage, move in the direction of the tip of your nose. At the end massage both sides of the nose. Then sense how the massage has made you feel like you are wearing a mask.
Sounding an 'n' into the mask	Now make an 'n' sound into this mask imagining that you are massaging your face internally through the sound. While doing this raise the corners of your mouth, as if you were grimacing.
Head on ground	Now kneel down on the ground and put your forehead and nose on a cloth or blanket. Make an 'n' sound as above, grimacing at the same time. In your imagination let the 'n'

flow from your back through your face into the ground.
Repeat this several times for as long as it feels comfortable.

Finishing exercise   Sense how you feel after the exercise for a moment. Then slowly move your buttocks to your heels and let your head hang. Then straighten your spine, vertebra by vertebra. Your head should straighten up at the end.

Functional level:
Circulation of sinuses (often recurrent sinus inflammations occur with vocal disorders).
Forward seat of the voice. Width in the vocal tract.
Improvement of the body's vibration capacity.

Personal level:
All the mucous membranes of the body react notably to psychological events. In this exercise not only does the nose begin to run, but everything else can begin to flow again.
A further reaction to this exercise may be that thinking becomes clearer and easier.

EXERCISE 20: Relaxing in the throat region

Sitting	Sit on the front third of a chair. Legs as wide apart as your hips. Feet parallel to each other on the ground.
Open feet	Imagine a triangle on the soles of your feet. A line connects the ball of the big and little toes and two lines run backwards to the heel. Let any tension in your body flow out through this triangle.
Open pelvis	In your imagination draw lines between your two ischia and coccyx so that a triangle is formed on your pelvic floor. Imagine this triangle is an aperture.
Space in the throat area	Caress your neck with your hands from top to bottom several times. In your imagination link the two frontal ends of your collarbone that lie close to your throat and the opposite lying cervical vertebra with lines so that an imaginary triangle is formed through your neck. Then imagine how the opening of the triangle gets larger as the front line gets longer in both directions.
Flowing	Imagine energy flowing through your body. The energy travels from your head and flows through the triangles in your neck, pelvis and feet down into the ground. Sense the effect for a while and bring the exercise to a close by stretching and yawning.

Functional level:
This exercise should be conducted in cases where neck symptoms are unclear.
Relaxation of the laryngeal region.

Personal level:

On a personal level, openness in the laryngeal area touches the themes of 'opening oneself' and 'being porous'.

Actively counteracting muscular tension in this area will be particularly difficult, but it may be possible to dissolve it by using your imagination.

Mental training used for competitive athletes and therapy used for psychosomatic illnesses show the influence that imagination has on the body.

Experimenting with our imagination may lead us to use our energy in a different way. We no longer need to do everything actively, but can 'let the work be done for us'.

Breathing

EXERCISE 21: Quiet breathing

Lying down

Lie on your back on the floor. Arms resting at your sides with your hands resting on their edges.
Legs lying as wide apart as your hips.
Feet turned outwards resting in a relaxed position.
Close your eyes and perceive all the contact areas of your body.

Centring

Now concentrate on your middle, located beneath your navel and about the size of a hand in width. In order to do this, place your hands on your lower abdomen so that the tips of your fingers touch at this point. After a while imagine there is a link to the sacrum that lies opposite it. Imagine a connecting line that runs through your body from front to back.
Then in your imagination connect these two points with a line that runs around your body. This line forms the upper rim of a bowl that extends to the pelvic floor.

Perceive the rhythm of your breathing

Observe how this imaginary bowl moves in tune with the rhythm of your breathing. It becomes wider when you inhale and narrower when you exhale.

Differentiating between breathing phases

In your imagination follow the three different breathing phases, each of which has a different significance.
– OUT:
While exhaling with a 'ff' let all your tension, feelings and thoughts flow from your head to your feet through your body.
Experience how you ultimately become empty.
– PAUSE:
Observantly wait for the ensuing breathing pause.

– IN:
Experience how the impulse to inhale sets in
again and enjoy the feeling of expansion in
your body as a whole.

Finishing exercise   Put your arms by your sides again and sense
what you feel before stretching to end the
exercise.

Functional level:

Stimulating deep breathing. Maximum mobility of diaphragm,
preparation of support, strength from pelvic area. Deep position of
the larynx.

Personal level:

To be conscious of ourselves and to accompany our own breathing
rhythm in our thoughts allows us to turn in on ourselves and
experience that we are also in sync with a rhythm that constitutes
all life. Inhalation signifies the will to live, exhalation to let go, and
pause for trust.

To allow ourselves to be carried by this rhythm without intervening
is something that we often find difficult. As we are accustomed to
'doing everything ourselves', we do not just simply let the breathing
occur, but intervene by breathing wilfully. However, if we manage
to allow ourselves to go along with our own and very personal
breathing rhythm without interrupting it we achieve a tranquillity
and composure that we can otherwise only achieve with difficulty.

EXERCISE 22: Expansion of breathing areas

Lying down

Lie on your back on the floor. Arms resting at your sides with your hands resting on their edges.
Legs lying as wide apart as your hips.
Feet turned outwards resting in a relaxed position.
Close your eyes and perceive all the contact areas of your body.

Raising legs

Let your legs rise, imagining that they are being pulled upwards by a thread, so that both soles of your feet are next to each other on the ground.

Arms bent

Bending your arms, rest them next to your head, like babies often do.

Legs to the side

Move your closed legs slowly to the left and put them on the floor. Sense how your right side is stretched. Then return to the starting position.
Repeat these actions again.

Crossed legs to the side

Cross your right leg over your left and move your crossed legs to the left.
Keep your legs as close to the ground as you can without your shoulders leaving the ground.

Lie on your side

Lie on your right side with your legs bent.
Place your left hand underneath your upper ribs. Using these ribs exert pressure on the hand. Sound an 'e' while doing this.
Then move your hand down to the next part of your costal arch, working through the whole of your rib area in the same way.

Compare

Lie on your back and compare your two sides. Then work through the other side in the same way.

Finishing exercise   Remain lying on your back for a while and be conscious of your breathing.

Functional level:
Activation of breathing through stretching of the intercostal muscles. Regulating of tension in the chest, improvement of body resonance.

Personal level:
To give ourselves space to breathe may give us the feeling of experiencing release in our chest and our whole self gains more space.
In order to bring about an optimal state of breathing, breathing space needs to be maximised. Bad posture accompanied by tension prevents the diaphragm from sinking and the muscles between the ribs from expanding.

EXERCISE 23: Perceiving reflex breath completion

Standing

Stand on both feet and concentrate on the contact area of your feet in relation to the floor.
Then stand on one foot and flex your leg, observing the effect it has on your whole body. Repeat the same action with your other leg.
To end with, be conscious of your whole body in its upright state.

Discovering the effect of intention

In a standing position, raise both arms mechanically several times, as if you were a robot. During this procedure be conscious of your body.
Then make the same arm movements, but with the intention of being a conductor giving the cue to an orchestra.
Does your body feel any different when doing this?
How did your breathing react?

Experiment with 'stop'

Imagine that your neighbour keeps chickens and that they have got into your garden. Shoo them away by saying 'stop, stop, stop' and using the appropriate hand movements.
How were you breathing when you did this?
The amount of air you used probably increased reflexly.
Then experiment with your breathing by consciously inhaling audibly before every 'go'.
How do you feel when doing this?
Can you sense the difference compared to the previous reflex breath completion?

Functional level:
Perception of change in tonus through intention.
Sinking and inhalatory direction of the diaphragm.
Consciousness of relaxation movement.

Personal level:
This exercise shows the important role played by intention. If we transpose ourselves into a situation completely and no longer think of how we 'do' something, all partial breathing and vocal output actions adjust to each other optimally, without our having to do anything. Inhalation occurs reflexly and is inaudible.

A necessary precondition for intentional behaviour is being prepared for a particular situation or action on a cognitive and emotional level.

EXERCISE 24: Practising relaxation

Standing	Stand up straight alternately running the soles of your feet over the ground. Do this several times. Then stand with both soles of your feet firmly on the ground and perceive the posture of your whole body.
Adjusting	Mentally adjust yourself to the following situations. Try to lay particular emphasis on the spoken words. Perceive how your body tension changes in the process.
Level of sound	– blow out candle with a vigorous 'fff'; – demand silence with a 'ssh'. Let go after these sounds completely and observe the relaxation movement that your diaphragm makes.
Level of word	'Come on!' – egging someone on. 'Plop!' – a stone falls in the water. 'Whoosh!' – pushing a child on a swing. 'Ouch!' – something hurts. 'Stop!' – somebody is about to run across the road. 'Quiet!' – noise in front of the bedroom window. Make sure that you do not inhale audibly before speaking. Inhalation occurs automatically if you adjust to the situation correctly.

Functional level:
Intention results in an increase of tonus, sinking of diaphragm and thereby inhalation.
Experiencing reflex breath completion.
Being conscious of the influence that intentional conduct has on tonus and breathing.
Creation and dissolution of physiological valve tension.

Personal level:
This exercise is also concerned with the effect intention has on the process of breathing. Gasping for air or drawing in air, often in conjunction with speaking too fast and without pausing, is a habit many people have. This has many causes. If children imitate their parents, educators or teachers this may give rise to non-physiological breathing behaviour. Further factors are our hectic and stressful lives, bad posture, a lack of balanced tension, and lack of intention.
Regaining physiological breathing that we were endowed with at birth requires time and awareness.

EXERCISE 25: With words and sentences

Rooting	Stand on the balls of your feet and let yourself drop down on to your heels several times. While doing this sense how you feel and how you land back on the floor each time. Afterwards stand firmly and securely on both legs.
Call out	Imagine that you are standing in a train station and waving to someone who is just leaving on a train. Call out something to that person, for example: 'Goodbye'; 'Have a good trip'; 'Give me a call'; 'Send my love to Gran'. Try to immerse yourself in this vision. Make sure that you do not inhale wilfully or audibly. As experienced in the foregoing exercises, inhalation occurs automatically if the intention exists.
Exclamations in conjunction with phrases	Follow an exclamation with a short phrase or sentence, for example: 'Ouch! – That hurts!' 'Stop! – Can't you wait?' 'No! – I don't want to!' 'Really! – I suspected as much!' Experience how the air reflexly flows in after the exclamation, making itself available for the ensuing phrase without your having to inhale wilfully. Pay attention to reflex breath completion after the phrase.

Functional level:
Expansion of reflex breath completion to the level of words and phrases. Practising pausing and apportioning.
Getting to know your own intentional behaviour.

Personal level:
To make a firm statement means it is easier to relax, but poses a problem for many people because it is associated with 'aggression'. 'Aggression' is usually experienced as something negative and is therefore rejected. Exclamations like the ones described above sometimes do not seem to have the right power of conviction.

It is easier to perform these exercises if you keep in mind that they are just a playful way of trying out different modes of conduct. This allows you to discover your own potential. The person practising decides what is taken over into spontaneous language, because it involves their performing a change in conduct.

EXERCISE 26: Apportioning of texts

Preparation

Ideally, the following exercise should be conducted in the presence of a listener. Before you enter this real situation prepare yourself by rooting yourself in either a sitting or standing position.

Dictating

Dictations are particularly suitable for practising the apportioning of a text.

Take any text and imagine that you want to dictate it to a secretary. Make sure you remain constantly in touch with your secretary and that he or she can easily follow you. Allow the secretary (and yourself) time to pause. Do not gasp for breath or take in air. The action of looking over at your secretary already allows you to inhale.

Reading fairy tales out loud

If the opportunity of reading to a child is not given, read a fairy tale as an exercise. Imagine that a child is sitting in front of you. Do not be 'glued' to your book, but remain in constant contact with the child while you are reading.

Is the child listening attentively?

Is it possible that you are reading too quickly, over the child?

Apportion the text so that the lengths of phrases spoken are not too long, allowing your breathing to occur reflexly.

Reading a newspaper article out loud

Read a short excerpt from a newspaper to someone at the breakfast table. The text should be about something very important or funny, your intention being that you must communicate it to your partner. Watch out for relaxation pauses and be conscious of breath completion.

Functional level:
Increase of the level of difficulty of Breath Rhythm Timed Phonation adjusted to phonation. Increase in the length of sentences and the transition for use in spontaneous language.
Training of partner-oriented speech behaviour by assuming and maintaining intentional conduct.
Work on phonation runs parallel with this.

Personal level:
Conducting this exercise with a partner means that our contact behaviour becomes visible. Are we partner-oriented, that is, directing our full attention to the other person and away from ourselves? Or do we always withdraw into ourselves? Can we endure pauses or do we find it intolerable that nothing is happening? Do we really let go of the last sound? Or do we complicate the act of finding our breath again by clipping off, pushing away, whispering or drawing out the last sound of each sentence?
Using the experiences with this exercise as a basis, it is interesting to reflect on our contact behaviour and the way we handle pauses in other situations.
By the time the stage is reached where a fairy tale is read out loud, it becomes apparent how somebody deals with pauses. Life is breathed into a fairy tale by pauses, creating tension. Pauses not only occur where commas or full stops are placed in the text, but through the division of the text into meaningful phrases. Tolerating these pauses proves to be difficult in our fast-paced age. If we do not do this we ignore our own breathing rhythm, making it difficult for the listener to get into the rhythm of listening that actually makes the difference to the atmosphere of the fairy tale.
The preparation at the beginning of the exercise is therefore very important in setting the conditions of inner calmness and 'getting across' the message to others at the same time.

EXERCISE 27: Consciousness of countertension

Walking	Walk upright around the room for a while. Consciously exert a little counterpressure against the floor with every step you take. Then stand firmly on both legs.
Drawing the 'bow'	Take a step forward with one leg and hold an imaginary bow in one hand in front of your body. With the other hand arch the bow (it is easier if you do in actual fact have a bow).
Release tension	Now slowly release the tension of the bow, sounding an 'o' at the same time. Repeat this action several times.
Drawing the bow with an 'o'	Now draw the bowstring again, but sound an 'o' when drawing back the string. Also repeat this action several times.
Compare	Alternate between both actions: sounding an 'o' when drawing the string and then when letting go of it. Can you tell a difference? When is it easier to make the sound? When can you hold the sound longest?

Functional level:
Restrained emission of air through maintaining inspiratory countertension.
Structure and consciousness of intention.
Not 'support' but 'elastic breathhold' (Coblenzer, 1987: 73).

Personal level:
In a narrower sense support is something that is learnt and is a form of breathing behaviour that is purpose-related. Singers have to train themselves to perform this function in order to be able to sustain the length of notes that are laid down in a composition.
In a further sense we talk of a supported sound in instances when the necessary tension is maintained. In particular, this occurs in response

to the intention of what we want to say and also through consciously assuming an intentional body posture.

On a personal level the themes of presence and openness are
touched upon.

EXERCISE 28: Sounding into the pelvis

Sitting as if anchored	Sit upright on the front third part of a chair and close your eyes. Anchor yourself with your feet in the ground and your buttocks on the seat of the chair. Experience your pelvis as a bowl in which you are sitting relaxed.
Breath out to the toneless sound 'hu'	Breath out a 'hu' without producing a vocal sound. It may help to imagine wind rushing through a forest.
'Filling' the pelvis	Now direct the 'hu' into your pelvis, imagining that you are filling it with this sound. This causes your pelvis to expand in all directions. Then 'colour' the 'hu' with some sound. Again, imagining the howling of the wind may help.
Sounding	Eventually the 'u' becomes increasingly audible in a deeper voice register. The 'h' sound is just a starting point. Fill your pelvic area with this tone. Make sure you do not exaggerate the rhythm of your breathing. Let go of the tone at the right time, allowing breath completion to occur reflexly. Enjoy the feeling of your inner organs being massaged as a result of the vibration caused.
Sensing	Sit still for a while and sense how the vibration in your body has had an effect. Then slowly end the exercise by stretching.

Functional level:
Restrained emission of air by maintaining inspiratory countertension.
'Elastic breathhold' (Coblenzer, 1987) instead of support.
Regulation of tonus through massaging from the inside. Improvement of vibration capability and resonance of the body.

Personal level:
This exercise causes intensive stimulation of the pelvic area and acts like a 'massage from the inside'.
It allows us to experience the effect of how vibration simultaneously relaxes and stimulates our whole body.
This exercise shows the paradox of support. When we inhale our breathing space normally expands and when we exhale it diminishes. However, the aim of support is to ensure maximum breathing space during voice output.
Imagining filling this space with a sound causes this to happen without the use of muscle tension.
This means that supportive breathing is experienced as elastic breathhold.

Phonation

EXERCISE 29: Yawning exercise

Sitting as if anchored	Sit upright on the front third part of a chair and close your eyes. Anchor yourself with your feet in the ground and your buttocks on the seat of the chair. Experience your pelvis as a bowl in which you are sitting relaxed.
Caressing the face	Caress your face with the palms of your hands from top to bottom and remember to let your lower jaw drop.
Imagining a ball of air	Imagine a ball of air in the cavity of your mouth is slowly increasing in size like a balloon. Perceive how your lower jaw drops lower and lower, and then expect to yawn.
Yawning	Let yourself yawn in a liberating manner. Your yawn should be neither a stifled polite yawn nor one that tears your mouth wide open.
Being conscious of your body expanding	Perceive how your body also expands through the action and savour the feeling.

Functional level:
Maximum use of resonance space brought about through expansion in the vocal tract coupled with low position of the larynx. This causes the primary laryngeal tone to be strengthened.

Personal level:
In our culture it is often considered to be improper to yawn heartily. This is the reason why many people have extreme difficulty in allowing this natural impulse of the body to occur, even when it is just an exercise. You must learn to accept this resistance and seek ways of overcoming it.
Themes that may arise:
losing control;
giving up roles (for example: lady, boss);
the ability to act naturally;
experiencing liberation.

EXERCISE 30: Drinking exercise

Sitting as if anchored	Sit upright on the front third part of a chair and close your eyes. Anchor yourself with your feet in the ground and with your buttocks on the seat of the chair. Experience your pelvis as a bowl in which you are sitting relaxed.
Caress face	Caress your face with both palms of your hands from top to bottom and remember to let your lower jaw drop.
Comparison swallowing – yawning	Swallow several times and be conscious of how this action causes your mouth and throat area to narrow. Then try yawning and be conscious of how this action causes the areas to widen. Alternate between yawning and swallowing, experimenting with the changing relation of space.
Drinking air	Cup your hands as if you wanted to scoop water from a spring. Lift your hands to your mouth and 'drink' the air that is in your hands. While doing so observe how your mouth and throat widen.
Yawning space when mouth is closed	Close your mouth at the end of the 'drinking phase' without losing its spaciousness. Make sure that no tension occurs while doing this.

Functional level:
Creating and becoming aware of space in the vocal tract. Improved perception of how the vocal tract changes when consonants are formed.

Personal level:
Allowing space in the cavity of our mouth may give us a feeling of looking unintelligent. If we stand in front of the mirror we can reassure ourselves that this is not the case. We can experiment with

the way it looks when the lower jaw is tensed or is pressed too far down and what the natural relaxed position is like. Similar themes to those addressed in Exercise 29 arise.

Releasing tension in the jaw can be a decisive step on the path to achieving new vocal behaviour.

EXERCISE 31: Humming

You will need a small stick for this exercise.

Sitting	Sit on the front third part of a chair. Legs as wide apart as your hips. Feet parallel to each other on the ground. Be conscious of the contact of your body with the chair and the floor and feel centred around your middle.
Feeling face and neck	Make yourself conscious of your face and your neck by touching them with a small stick. Starting with the right side of your face, feel its features in the following order: forehead; eye and cheekbone; one side of nose; ear; cheek; one side of mouth; chin; neck and nape.
Compare	Now compare the right side that you have felt with the left. What differences can you detect? Then feel the left side in the same way and compare again.
Caress face	Then caress your face with both hands from top to bottom letting your lower jaw drop. Try to bring about a gentle yawning through this action. Placing both hands on your face, feel outwards from within: the skin of your face feels your hands.
Finding physiological pitch	Imagine that you are tired, lying in bed and really want to go to sleep, but your partner is talking to you and you politely say 'hmm' from time to time.

Humming	Extend the 'hmm' until you start humming. Whilst you are humming feel your face and your head and be conscious of where you can feel a vibration.
Perceiving body vibration	Continue to hum and gently thump your chest with your fists and be conscious of the vibration. Carry on humming and try to let the vibration run through your whole body down to your feet.
Sensing	Sit still for a while longer and feel how the vibration in your body has taken effect. Then slowly end the exercise by stretching.

Functional level:
Stimulation of vibratory function of vocal fold mucosa. Achieving complete body resonance. Discovery of the intermediate position.

Personal level:
To sound a neutral 'hmm' is the surest way of finding our own personal vocal pitch. There are situations in which we run the risk of speaking in a pitch that is too high, putting strain on the voice. For example, on the telephone, giving a lecture, and so on. A discreet 'hmm' before these situations can help us find our physiological speaking voice register. Vocal pitch when speaking may serve as a kind of barometer that indicates inner tension. Through regulating it consciously we can influence our entire state of tension.

Humming is also the best way of dealing with the urge to clear your throat. Through the action of the vocal fold vibration, troublesome mucus is transported away.

EXERCISE 32: Chewing exercise

You will need a dry bread roll for this exercise.

Sitting	Sit on the front third part of a chair. Legs as wide apart as your hips. Feet parallel to each other on the ground. Be conscious of your ischia and the solid connection of your feet to the ground. Centre yourself in your middle.
Chewing	Take a bite from a dry bread roll. Perceive how far you automatically open your mouth to perform this action. Now chew the bitten off piece slowly, savouring it, and concentrate on the chewing motion. Perceive the tension in the mouth and jaw muscles and the extent of jaw motion. Repeat this chewing action several times.
Chewing and humming	Now make a chewing motion with nothing in your mouth and hum an 'm'. Perceive the vibrations caused when sounding this 'm' and be conscious of the change in tonus that occurs with the changed distance of the jaws.
Chewing syllables	Now sound syllables while you are chewing: 'mjam, mjem, mjim, mjom, mjum, njam, njem, njim ...' Sense the way in which you fill your mouth with the spoken syllables and be conscious of the pitch that you are speaking in.
Transfer to words	Now make the transfer from chewed syllables to words, for example, days of the week or names of months. Be conscious of the way your articulatory organs move.

Functional level:
Easing of the throat area.
Improvement of articulation, creating jaw space, forward projection of the position of sound.

Personal level:
Chewing with an open mouth conflicts with our cultural norms. It is considered, among other things, unattractive to chew with an open mouth. There is something animalistic and aggressive about chewing and biting, these actions are linked to our instinctuality and aggressivity.

EXERCISE 33: Vowel spaces

Lying and centring Lie on your back on the floor. Legs lying as wide apart as your hips. Feet turned outwards resting in a relaxed position. Your hands on your lower stomach, with your fingertips touching at about a hand's width below your navel. Centre yourself by feeling into yourself.

Being conscious of breathing rhythm Be conscious of your breathing rhythm and follow it in your thoughts:
out = let go;
pause = wait;
in = let it happen.

Vowel 'u' Breathe out audibly with a quiet, deep 'hu'. The tone is just begun with the 'h', so it is barely audible. Relax at the correct time and breathe in reflexly. Fill your abdominal-pelvic area with the 'u' sound and feel how your organs are massaged in this area.

Vowel 'o' Caress the whole of the centre of your body with your hands, the areas that would usually be covered by a motorcyclist's belt. Then send an 'o' in this area as described above and massage all the organs located there with the vibration.

Vowel 'e' Caress your chest and neck several times with your hands and then sound an 'e' in this area. Your voice will probably become a little higher than when sounding an 'o' and a 'u'. Accompany your voice experimenting with different pitch levels in order to discover which one allows you to fill your chest area with an 'e' most easily.

Vowel 'i' Send an 'i' into your head and also experiment to find out the correct pitch.

Vowel 'a'	Imagine that you are lying in a big 'A'. The point of the letter is above your head, the two shafts of the 'A' run along your sides. Fill the space around your body with an 'a' tone and again find the most comfortable pitch.
Sensing	For a little while longer sense how your body feels now. Stretch slowly, with your limbs close to your body as if you were making this movement under a blanket. Then slowly assume a sitting position via your side.

Functional level:
Eutonus throughout the whole body. Stimulates body resonance.

Personal level:
This exercise involves taking a step further in working on the body and breathing. The first step led us to regulating tonus via bodily self-perception. Through centring and observing our breathing we then discovered our own rhythm. A further step was taken by sounding into the body, which led to experiencing ourselves in vibration. The effect on our physical, psychological and mental state can be as diverse as people are. Being conscious of the effect and thinking about it is essential.

EXERCISE 34: Directional sounding of tones

Sitting as if anchored	Sit upright on the front third part of a chair and close your eyes. Anchor yourself with your feet in the ground and with your buttocks on the seat of the chair. Experience your pelvis as a bowl in which you are sitting relaxed.
Caress face	Caress your face with both palms of your hands from top to bottom and remember to let your lower jaw drop.
Feeling space in the cavity of your mouth	With your mouth closed move your tongue: up so that it touches your hard palate; down feeling the floor of your mouth; into the cheeks feeling the inner walls of your cheeks; forward, behind your closed lips; and lastly visualise the back part of the cavity of your mouth, where soft palate and uvula are located. The movements should be done in a playful manner, so that the muscles involved do not become tense.
Sounding tones into the mouth	Sound an 'm' and let it radiate to the different points of your mouth. Imagine directing it upwards to begin with and then downwards, and so on.
Filling the cavity of the mouth with sound	Then imagine the 'm' spreading in all directions simultaneously. Imagining a balloon expanding slowly may help to visualise this.
Sounding tones into the body	Now send the 'm' into the different parts of your body: down into your feet; up into your head; to the right into your right side; to the left into your left side; to the front into your front half; to the back into your back half.

Functional level:
Creating space in the vocal tract. Achieving and being conscious of entire body resonance.
Taking pressure off the larynx – not with the larynx, but 'through' it.

Personal level:
Some people find that when they do this exercise it is the first time that they become conscious of the full capacity of their voice, which can trigger off deep emotional shock. Beautiful vocal sound does not always result in a pleasant experience. It can also be connected with that to which we are excitedly looking forward. Or the fear of how much of the self is exposed 'forces itself to the outside (sounds)'.

EXERCISE 35: With syllables

Sitting as if anchored	Sit upright on the front third part of a chair and close your eyes. Anchor yourself with your feet in the ground and with your buttocks on the seat of the chair. Experience your pelvis as a bowl in which you are sitting relaxed.
Caressing the face	Caress your face with both palms of your hands from top to bottom and remember to let your lower jaw drop.
Humming	Locate your physiological speaking pitch by sounding an impartial 'mh'. Draw this 'mh' out until you begin to hum. Be conscious of how your whole body starts to vibrate.
Humming with syllables	Combine the 'mh' with the vowels 'o' or 'u', for example: 'mom – momomom, momomu, mumu'. Make sure that your lips are protruding slightly and that you can move them easily. Then continue by starting with the 'm' sound, but letting the sound of the added vowel linger on its own: 'mooo, muuu, maaa'. Try the same with the consonant 'n'.
Syllables in physiological speaking pitch	Imagine that the smell of your favourite food is wafting through the house and, with appetite, say 'mh'. Starting with this (spoken) 'mh' put vowels on the end: 'mom, mum, momomum' and so on. Also try this with 'n' and in conjunction with all vowels. Exaggerate the formation of the nasal sounds of 'm' and 'n', in order to make your voice sound.

Syllables with
modulation

Using an imaginary partner, conduct a conversation consisting of syllables. Try doing this using different moods, for example, happy, angry, questioning, and so on. Let your voice resonate as richly as possible.

Functional level:
Stabilisation of physiological speaking voice pitch.
Creation of resonance spaces.
Forward projection of the position of sound.

Personal level:
This exercise is about discovering your own sound potential.
To draw your own voice out you need to exaggerate your voice. We can assume that our voice is already there, which means that nothing new really needs to be acquired. Our voice is, however, often hidden or distorted or has not got the courage to emerge. Or we produce it with force. To picture this: we violently force it through a narrow space in a door instead of flinging the door wide open.
In this exercise we can compare ourselves to an instrument (for example, a large cello) where sound occurs of its own accord. What we need to do is to be like a cello; to open ourselves up and to have the courage to let our sound ring out.

EXERCISE 36: With words

Swinging to and fro Stand up straight and concentrate on the contact of the soles of your feet with the ground.
Perceive the gentle movement of your body that is caused by breathing, although you appear to be standing completely still. Go along with this movement; increase it until you eventually swing from a forward to a backward position. Find your own rhythm. Make sure that your lower jaw is relaxed.

Humming While continuing to swing, find your physiological speaking pitch by sounding an impartial 'mh' until you find yourself humming. Add different vowels to the 'm' and experiment with different resonance possibilities.

Syllables in physiological speaking pitch Stand up and make the transition to experimenting with syllables in a vocal pitch: 'mom, mumumom', and so on.
Direct these syllables into the room or towards an (imaginary) partner.
Follow this 'directing of syllables' with a corresponding hand movement.

Using words Direct words beginning with 'm' or 'n' – 'moon', 'middle', mast', 'name', and so on – into the room in the same way.
While you do this, exaggerate the pronunciation of the consonant at the beginning of the word to bring about complete body resonance.
With every word you pronounce, can you feel your body vibrating right through to your feet?

Word chains   String words together that all begin with the letter 'm' or 'n'. These 'sentences' do not have to make sense. Experiment thoroughly with words and 'bathe' in the sound of them.

Functional level:
Stabilisation of the physiological speaking voice pitch.
Creation of resonance spaces.
Transfer into speaking voice.

Personal level:
Experimenting with our richly resonant voice on the level of words takes us a step further towards the transfer of our sound potential, to speaking. We may find that the desire to form a new kind of vocal behaviour is triggered, but resistance may also be provoked. It is important to be conscious of the feelings that are connected with the newly discovered voice.

This exercise involves speaking in a voice that is unusually deep and has an exaggerated resonance. This allows us to develop our voice to its full potential.

EXERCISE 37: Series of words and sentences

Standing	Stand on both feet and concentrate on the contact area of your feet with the floor. Then stand on one foot and flex your leg. While doing this observe the effect it has on your whole body. Repeat the same with your other leg. Then be conscious of your whole body in its upright posture.
Setting off resonance	Set off resonance by sounding an impartial 'mh' find your vocal pitch and experiment with resonance possibilities using syllables on 'mom', 'mum', and so on. Move on to words that begin with 'm' or 'n'.
Stringing series of words together – days of the week and names of months	Pronounce the word 'Monday' several times with exaggerated resonance. Then carry on counting down the days of the week: 'Tuesday', 'Wednesday', and so on. Carry over the resonance of the word 'Monday' to the other words. Try the same with the names of the months, but start with 'May' in order to bring about resonance more easily.
Stringing sentences together	String sentences together that all start with the same word and with the letter 'm' or 'n', for example: 'My mother is cooking.' 'Molly is cooking.' 'Molly is sleeping.' You will always find your way back to your resonant voice through the initial sound, which you then maintain for everything that follows.

Functional level:
Maintaining complete body resonance when the transition into spontaneous language is made.

Personal level:
This exercise brings us very close to our use of spontaneous language. We have now become more familiar with our richer voice through the foregoing exercises and maybe we have carried something over into our spontaneous language without our having consciously striven to do so. The step that needs to be taken is sometimes a difficult one. On the one hand, we may be happy about our newly discovered voice; on the other hand, we become conscious that the change in voice behaviour means a general change in conduct. Questions may arise such as:
How will my relationship with other people change if I no longer speak in my little, timid voice?
Will other people find me too self-confident or even aggressive?
Or even:
Will my colleagues still accept me as a boss if my voice has become softer?

If we experience any resistance to using the 'new' voice, it may be due to this kind of insecurity. It is important that we take them seriously and understand them. At this stage practice on its own will not suffice.

EXERCISE 38: Consciousness of the position of sound

Sitting as if anchored	Sit up straight on the front third part of a chair and close your eyes. Anchor yourself with your feet in the ground and with your buttocks on the seat of the chair. Experience your pelvis as a bowl in which you are sitting relaxed.
Caress face	Caress your face with both palms of your hands from top to bottom and remember to let your lower jaw drop.
Creating yawning space	Be conscious of the space in the cavity of your mouth. With your mouth closed, try and yawn silently. Now sense how much space has been created in the cavity of your mouth.
Perceive the position of sound	Repeat the word 'cuckoo' several times and be conscious of where you form these sounds in your mouth. Then say 'kitty', and again take conscious note. Which of the two words can you feel more at the back of your mouth and which at the front? Alternate pronouncing both words, to refine your perception of the position of the sound.
Frontal position of the sound	Now say both words after each other: 'kitty's cuckoo'. Be conscious of how the word 'cuckoo', which you could feel at the back, has now shifted to the front.
Experimenting with position of sounds	Try this shifting forward of sounds with other words. For example, say 'cauliflower' as far back in your throat as possible, as if you wanted to swallow the word. Then say it as far forward in your mouth as you can, as if you wanted to flick the word out.

Try the same with numbers. First form the words right at the back of your throat and then towards the front. Choose an opposite lying wall as the direction you are targeting and imagine that these numbers are meant to hit it.

Functional level:

Exercise designed for throaty voices.

Experimenting with tension and spatial change in the vocal tract.

Bringing the dorsally projected position of sound forward.

Personal level:

If your voice sits predominantly in your throat area it quickly tires and it also becomes difficult for people to understand what you are saying, it therefore becomes necessary to experiment with the position of sound.

Bringing the voice forward touches on themes such as coming out of one's shell, getting something 'across' to others and being partner-oriented.

EXERCISE 39: Use of vowels

Sitting as if anchored	Sit up straight on the front third part of a chair and close your eyes. Anchor yourself with your feet in the ground and with your buttocks on the seat of the chair. Experience your pelvis as a bowl in which you are sitting relaxed.
Creating yawning space	Let your lower jaw drop and create yawning space in the cavity of your mouth.
Perceiving valve tone	Whisper the sentence: 'Ann and Alan are angry'. Perceive how each vowel begins with a little, clean bang. Now repeat all the initial sounds 'A-a-a-ann a-a-a-and A-a-a-alan a-a-a-are a-a-a-angry.' Listen to the delicate 'little valve tone' which occurs when the vowels are formed.
Use of vowels with syllables	In a whisper, repeat the initial sound of a syllable again, but then let the next syllable voice itself of its own accord. So, for example: Whisper 'o-o-o' with voice 'om'
	'u-u-u' 'usch'
	'a-a-a' 'af'
With words	Try to do the same with words: Whispering 'o-o-o' using your voice 'often';
	'e-e-e' 'east'
	'a-a-a' 'after'
	Imagine that your vowels are dripping from a leaking tap, like drops of water.

Functional level:
Trying out different methods of vocal attack.
Realising a physiological vocal attack.
Closure of the glottis.

Personal level:
When using vowels you can hear when too much or too little energy is being expended. Vowels require special attention if they are too hard or 'rasping'. Pressure on the laryngeal valve can be a sign of internal pressure.

It is extremely difficult to make the transition from a practice situation to spontaneous language. Through practice you can merely discover the position of tension, in which a physiological vocal attack is possible. It may be helpful to imagine listening to your own voice production with a sense of amazement or taking a wait-and-see attitude.

The exercise with vowels requires us to let something happen without our wanting to intervene and do it ourselves.

EXERCISE 40: Final syllables

Sitting as if anchored	Sit upright on the front third part of a chair and close your eyes. Anchor yourself with your feet in the ground and with your buttocks on the seat of the chair. Experience your pelvis as a bowl in which you are sitting relaxed.
Creating yawning space	Let your lower jaw drop and create yawning space in the cavity of your mouth.
Filling the cavity of your mouth with sound	Hum an 'm'. Imagine that the 'm' is spreading simultaneously everywhere in your mouth. The picture of a balloon expanding slowly may help you to imagine this.
Serving up final syllables with a hand motion	In a clearly resonant voice pronounce words that end in 'en', like 'strengthen', 'tighten', shorten', and so on. Pay attention to the final syllables. Can they be understood and do they sound melodious, or does the resonance get lost? Repeat the same words, accompanying them with a motion of the hand as if you wanted to serve them up to a conversation partner. With your hand extended, listen to the sound of the final syllables for a little longer.
Perceiving differences	Now consciously drop the voice sound of the final syllables. Repeat the same words, but when pronouncing the final syllables stop standing up straight. Your back slumps. Be conscious of the change in voice sound. Remaining seated in an upright position, repeat the words as above with the accompanied hand motion. Alternate between both possibilities until you have become completely aware of the difference between them.

Functional level:
Upholding of intentional tension curve.
Giving a definite end to a phrase of speech.
Maintaining resonance space.

Personal level:
Unintelligible or grating final syllables arise if tension is not upheld to the end of what is being said. The voice retreats, and whether the speaker also has a tendency to retreat should be considered.
Themes that may arise:
Taking oneself and what one is saying seriously.
Being partner-oriented, present.

EXERCISE 41: Increasing sound level

Standing

Stand up straight and concentrate on the contact of the soles of your feet with the ground. Then stand on the balls of your feet and let yourself drop back on to your heels. By doing so, get in touch with yourself and the floor.

Humming

Locate your physiological speaking pitch by sounding an impartial 'mh' until you find yourself humming. Add different vowels to the 'm' and experiment with different resonance possibilities: 'mom, mumumum', and so on.

Filling space with sound

With a motion of the hand, send these syllables into the room. Fill the room with 'pockets of sound'. Then do the same with syllables in your speaking pitch.

Using words'

Direct words beginning with 'm' or 'n' – 'moon', 'middle', 'mast', 'name', and so on – into the room in the same way.
While doing this, exaggerate the pronunciation of the consonant at the beginning of the word to bring about complete body resonance.
With every word you pronounce, can you feel your body vibrating right through to your feet?

Using sentences

Form sentences with words that all start with the letter 'm' or 'n'. The sentences do not necessarily have to make sense. Experiment properly with all the words and 'bathe' in their sound.

From a distance

Now imagine that somebody is standing far away from you. Try to reach this person with your sonorous word.
While doing this, imagine your body is gradually expanding.

Functional level:
Opening up resonance space.
Improving the capacity of the voice through an increase of space.
Increase of sound level.

Personal level:
An increase in the level of sound does not arise from an increased use of energy in the laryngeal area, but through the expansion of the resonance space. In order to achieve this we need to make our whole body available, as an instrument. However, as people we often withdraw to such an extent, take up insufficient space, that our body only remains present in a diminished form. This exercise enables us to gain the courage to attain our own voice and discover that it is a pleasurable experience to let the voice ring out.

EXERCISE 42: Modulation

Standing or Sitting   Stand or sit up straight, establishing a good connection to the floor or chair.
Be conscious of your body and centre yourself.

Gliding tones   Let your voice glide down with a sigh of relief. Then let your voice glide up again. Imagine a lift going up. At the same time draw your hand down in front of your body.
Your voice should glide from one tone into another uninterruptedly.

Modulating with vowels   Imagine different situations in which you express yourself with the use of exclamations made with vowels, for example:
'a' – amazement;
'i' – disgust;
'o' – surprise.
Pay attention to the range of tones your voice covers while doing this.

With words and sentences   Say a word like 'yesterday' or 'always' to yourself in a soft and monotonous tone. Then imagine a specific situation and use the word expressing a particular mood, for example shock, scepticism or happiness.
Try the same thing with a sentence like:
'What do you want?'
Exaggerate the way you express yourself and be conscious of how your voice moves through different pitches while you do this.

Functional level:
Perception and improvement of prosodic elements:
stresses on words or sentences;
dynamics (soft–loud);
melodiousness (low–high);
rhythm (slow–fast).

Personal level:
It is not only information that is communicated via language, but also sentiment. Using a monotonous voice means that we are unlikely to reach our speaking partner, let alone convince that person of what we are saying. Monotony is something that is not only tiresome to a partner, but is tiring for one's own voice and it signifies a lack, or inappropriateness, of intention.

Some people are consciously soft-spoken and monotonous in order to appear demure, but the effect they have is the exact opposite. In order for their conversation partner to be able to understand exactly what they are saying they need to give the speaker their full attention.

Working on the voice's capacity to modulate touches upon emotional expression, which is often suppressed by people because they are afraid of getting hurt.

EXERCISE 43: Calling voice

Standing	Stand on the balls of your feet and let yourself drop on to your heels several times. Experience how you get in touch with yourself and the ground every time you do this. Then stand firmly and securely on both legs.
Diaphragmatic impulses	Say 'st' or 'pst' resolutely as if you want to attract attention. Be conscious of the way your diaphragm moves. Hold one nostril closed and expel air from the other in short, powerful bursts, as if you are attempting to clear your nose.
With sound	With your mouth wide open, now let your voice sound in the same powerful bursts. Gradually transform this vocal sound into a short 'ho'.
Shouting	Then shout 'ho-ho-ho', without holding your nose. Perceive the way your diaphragm moves. Add a word to the 'ho', for example: 'ho-ho-hold!' 'ho-ho-hi!' Then omit the 'ho' and shout names. Make sure that the impulse still emanates from the diaphragm. Now shout something that you yourself would normally shout in the same way, for example, 'Phone!', 'Dinner!'

Functional level:
Strengthening of subglottal pressure.
Impulse from deep down.
Jolting relaxation of the diaphragm which causes mechanical irritation to the muscles that pull the larynx down.
Flexible diaphragm.

Personal level:
This exercise effectively trains the diaphragm muscles. It is also important for people who have to speak in a loud voice (teachers, parents, dog owners, and so on). This exercise can also become a new experience for everyone who does not yet have the courage to use their own voice.
Themes that may arise:
fear of being too loud;
aggressivity;
allowing yourself to be noticed;
self-consciousness.

Articulation

EXERCISE 44: Formation of vowels

Sitting as if anchored	Sit upright on the front third part of a chair and close your eyes. Anchor yourself with your feet in the ground and with your buttocks on the seat of the chair. Experience your pelvis as a bowl in which you are sitting relaxed.
Caress face	Caress your face with both palms of your hands from top to bottom and remember to let your lower jaw drop.
Humming	Locate your physiological speaking pitch by sounding an impartial 'mh' until you find yourself humming. Be conscious of how your whole body starts to vibrate.
Forming vowels	Add the vowel 'o' on to 'm' and let it sound for a while: 'moh'. Perceive the shape that the cavity of your mouth and your lips assume. Then start again with 'moh' and slowly glide from the 'o' into an 'a': 'mohwa'. Make sure that the vowels both sound the same. Using the other vowels try the same thing. To end, go straight into the vowels without the preparatory 'o', for example, 'muu', 'mee', 'mii' and so on.

Functional level:
Maintaining resonance space while simultaneously changing the cavity of the mouth to form different vowels.
Balancing the vibrating mass of the vocal folds.

Personal level:
This exercise is particularly important for singing. Balancing vowels means that the same sound is maintained with different vowels, but the vowels can at the same time clearly be recognised from one another.

When speaking, it is also irksome if a vowel 'stands out' and, for example, an 'e' or 'ei' is pronounced too broadly.

What applies to all vowels (and sonant consonants) is that they make our voices audible, allowing our personal sound to emerge.

EXERCISE 45: Being conscious of consonant formation

Experiment	Picture yourself standing at a well and dropping a stone into it. Say 'plop'. Experiment with using the word in different ways: disinterestedly and a little sluggishly; a little stilted and exaggeratedly; observing the falling process with interest. Be conscious of the different way your mouth muscles work.
Thinking out loud	Imagine that you are packing a suitcase. In a soft voice list the items that need to go into the suitcase in order to help you think. Perceive how clearly the consonants are 'seized' without your having to do it deliberately.
Emphasising consonants	Slowly write a text in a large hand reading it out loud as you go along, as if you were a school beginner. Be conscious of the movement that your lips, tongue and whole mouth make.

Functional level:
Improvement of articulation through intention.
Improvement of consciousness of the articulatory realm.
Perception and training of unitary function of breathing–voice–articulation.

Personal level:
This exercise makes you aware of articulatory activity when consonants are formed. If intention is directed solely towards one event, the required tension will be brought about of its own accord. Consonants are also described as 'carriers of meaning'. This is particularly noticeable in the case of singing. If consonants are not well articulated, a beautiful voice may be audible but the sense of what is being sung is not conveyed to the listener.

EXERCISE 46: Speaking with a cork in your mouth
You will require a cork for this exercise.

Sitting	Sit upright on the front third part of a chair. Your feet are in firm contact with the ground. Centre yourself in your pelvis.
Reading	Read a text out loud in the way that you usually would. Be conscious of what your articulation is like.
With a cork in your mouth	Put a cork (or your thumb) between your incisors and read the same text. Be conscious of how active your articulatory muscles have to become if the text is to be intelligible.
After speaking with a cork in your mouth	Read the same text again without a cork in your mouth. Is the activity of your articulation muscles greater than it was with your first attempt at reading?

Functional level:
Improvement of articulation through intention.
Consciousness of the articulatory realm.
Forming of sounds when resistance exists.

Personal level:
In this exercise it becomes clear that forces can be mobilised through opposition.
With a cork between the teeth the text is only intelligible if the articulatory activity is increased. The tension that is built up is still maintained when the cork is taken away again.
This exercise is, however, only designed to make us aware of what our articulation is normally like and for discovering the possibilities that exist for clear articulation. If you speak for too long with a cork in your mouth there is the danger of too much tension being built up in the articulatory area.

EXERCISE 47: Forming of consonants

Standing	Stand up straight and concentrate on the contact of the soles of your feet with the ground. Then stand on the balls of your feet and let yourself drop back on to your heels. In this way land back on the floor and perceive how you feel.
Experimenting	Say the sentence 'I'm feeling fed up' in different ways: vocal-orientedly with almost incomprehensible consonants; consonant-orientedly with particular stress on the 'f' consonants, that is: 'I'm ffeeling ffed up.' When does this statement sound more convincing?
Becoming conscious of the articulatory muscles	Be conscious of the space in your mouth by feeling it with your tongue. Then experiment with what you can do with your tongue, for example, roll it up, stick it out, click it, and so on. What movements can you make with your lips? In which directions can you move your lower jaw?
Consonant-oriented speaking	Say a short sentence to an imaginary (or real) partner with emphasis or conviction, for example: 'Stop that immediately!' 'That's really good.' 'Mmm, that smells nice.' Relish the formation of the consonants.

Functional level:
Improvement of articulation through intention.
Consciousness of the articulatory realm.

Personal level:

'Mumbling' puts a strain on the listener because it forces the listener to pay full attention. It also strains the voice of the speaker because of the unitary function of breathing–voice–articulation.

The way in which we articulate ourselves expresses the way in which we want to inform and shape. In addition, it shows how important we think what we want to say is and therefore how seriously we take ourselves. Practising clearer articulation can increase our self-awareness, and we can experience being able to 'express' ourselves.

10
Suggestions for the Transfer

As described in Part I, in PVT the transfer is understood to be a conscious permanent process. People practising voice development need to be creative so that they may discover when or where their newly acquired discoveries can be practised or integrated into everyday life. The following is intended to offer some suggestions. Furthermore, we show how the levels of difficulty can be stepped up.

Transfer Exercises

Balance between Attention Directed Internally and Externally

Faced with outwardly directed performances and communicative situations there lies a danger of directing our attention away from ourselves.

The following exercise starts with bodily self-perception and ultimately moves outwards, without our losing sight of ourselves.

Sit upright on a chair, close your eyes and perceive your contact surfaces. When you sense that you are completely in touch with yourself, 'open' your ears and be conscious of what you can hear around you. Register the noises or sounds without identifying or evaluating them, for example, by being happy at the sound of birdsong, but being annoyed at the noise of building work. Try to accept all 'voices' as belonging to a large 'orchestra'.

Now open your eyes and to begin with direct your gaze at the ground. Are you able simultaneously to hear, see and perceive yourself as still sitting on the chair?

Eventually let your gaze wander around, taking in more and more of your surroundings. However, make sure that you always sense your self at the same time.

Increasing Level of Difficulty

Through gradual steps the newly acquired speech behaviour moves from being used in a practice situation to being used in spontaneous language: for example, in poems, fairy tales, lyrical prose, newspaper texts, pictorial descriptions, the telling of stories, controlled speaking situations and controlled conversations.

1. Poems.
   Because of their meter, poems are a good way of dividing the spoken word into phrases.
2. Fairy tales and lyrical prose.
   Pauses play a decisive role in the arrangement of fairy tales or lyrical prose. This makes them ideal texts for learning how to break up the text so that it is tune with our own breathing rhythm. They provide a good way for practising the task of 'enduring' pauses, which is often difficult to master. If we simultaneously employ the richness of our voice to the full we can experience ourselves as a vibrating 'instrument'.
3. Newspaper texts.
   Reading newspaper texts which are factual and more sober than fairy tales or lyrical prose means moving on to a higher level of difficulty. Reading a small section from a newspaper out loud every morning can become a customary way of inciting us to use our newly acquired speech behaviour on a daily basis.
4. Pictorial descriptions and telling stories.
   These involve using semi-spontaneous language, that is, the content is laid down but we are free to formulate it in any way that we choose.
5. Controlled speaking situations.
   These are speaking situations which are consciously brought about, the contents of which are brief and easy to comprehend, for example, a short telephone conversation, or at a shop counter, when making a purchase, and so on.
6. Controlled conversations.
   What is meant by this is conversations in which attention is paid not only to the content of what is being said and the response given, but also to which new vocal behaviour is consciously employed. Allowances should be made for interruptions and cor-

rections, but as a rule these should come from the person practising voice development. The conversation partner is aware that the conversation is a practice conversation.

Aids and Options for Transfer

Everyday situations can provide the practice field without taking up extra time (Dürckheim, 1985). The following are a few suggestions:

1. 'Letting off steam'.
   Be alert to tension and agitation in your body. If you are alone in a room, relieve tension that you are experiencing by audibly exhaling a 'ssh' or 'f'. It may be helpful to imagine opening the valve on a pressure cooker. Eventually you will be able to 'let off steam' without exhaling audibly, so that you can use it wherever you are.
2. Pauses to change gear.
   Work on pauses to readjust in which you can introduce an exercise into the routine of your life – a short break, for example, during lunch or after work where you withdraw and concentrate on yourself. A brief interruption or pause during work in which, for example, you step in front of an open window and practise bodily self-awareness or simply stretch.
   Walking can also provide a suitable pause to readjust. All errands that we have to run can be turned into an exercise by making ourselves aware of our contact in relation to the ground when we are walking. There is no need to put aside extra time in order to do this, but the effect on our condition can be remarkable.
3. Times when we have to wait.
   We can turn all waiting times into exercise times. It is amazing how much time we spend waiting in the course of our lives, and how annoying it is: for example, when waiting to pay for shopping: when waiting at the bank, the bus stop, the doctor's surgery or the airport; or waiting in the car during a traffic jam. Whether we are sitting or standing, we can make ourselves aware of our contact surfaces and thereby regulate our tonus. A further step can be to focus our concentration on our middle, that is, to centre ourselves and be conscious of our breathing rhythm. Having practised, we will become accustomed to doing this and it will then be easy to direct our attention to the outside world at the same time.

4. Cues.

A cue, even a coded one in the form of a picture or sign that is placed somewhere where we can often see it, can serve as a reminder for what we want to introduce into our everyday life.

A genuine transfer does not occur when we do something differently or new in our everyday lives, but when we have become different.

Part IV
Therapeutic Procedure in PVT

11
The Structure of Therapy

The structure of work on the voice in PVT orientates itself on the physiology of voice production. Eberle (1979) was the first person to break down this structure into categories.

Dividing and separating voice therapy into categories is, however, only possible on a theoretical level and merely serves the purpose of providing a better overview or sub-division for didactic reasons.

Figure 11.1 illustrates the basic structure for PVT.

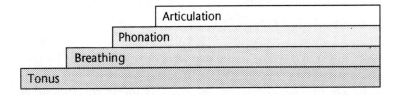

Figure 11.1

These categories consist of the following:

1. Tonus

- work on proprioception
- regulating tonus
- work on the spine
- work on the abdominal-pelvic area
- physiological posture when seated, standing or walking
- relaxing neck, nape and shoulder muscles
- loosening and sensitisation of articulation and phonation areas.

165

2. Breathing

- perceiving breathing rhythm and breathing spaces
- achieving reflex breath completion
- achieving Breath Rhythm Timed Phonation
- achieving inspiratory countertension.

3. Phonation

- creating resonance space in the vocal tract
- achieving physiological speaking pitch
- achieving complete body resonance
- work on the position of sound
- work on vocal fold ad- and abduction
- improvement of voice dynamics
- improvement of modulation capability.

4. Articulation

- formation of vowels
- formation of consonants.

From this sketch it can be seen that work on the body is the basis for the entire work within PVT (compare Chapter 2, pp. 20–25). Transfers into the other categories should be fluent. For example, an exercise which is intended to improve articulation is not separable from intonation, which also makes it a phonation exercise. This in turn requires breathing, which requires regulated tonus. This makes an articulation exercise an exercise involving all categories.

12
Conducting the Exercises

Selecting an Exercise

There are different approaches to selecting exercises:

1. Structure of a physiological function according to individual
   therapy structure steps.
   The structure of a new vocal pattern is based upon the functional
   structure of the different components of vocal output. Individual
   steps must be carried out one after the other. So, for example, it
   only makes sense to work on phonation when costal abdominal
   breathing has been achieved; a condition of which is elastic
   tonus.

   Usually it is not necessary to conduct exercises from all the
   categories in the case of every client. So, for example, there may
   be no need to work on a client's articulation since there is
   nothing wrong with it. Or developing the desired frontal position
   of sound may have such a positive influence on the use of vowels
   that there is no particular need to work on it.

2. The client's symptoms.
   The choice of exercises will also be determined by the symptoms
   the client has. The more understanding the therapist has of the
   client's symptoms the easier it will be to select an exercise.
   Proceeding along the lines of 'What do you do with which voice
   disorder?' is an approach that may sometimes prove to be unpro-
   ductive since the symptom may be so different that it cannot be
   categorised within the framework. It makes more sense for a
   therapist to use his or her own perception to arrive at ideas for
   therapy. This can, for example, be done if the therapist tries
   imitating the symptoms of a client when preparing for a sitting.

Kinaesthetic perception sometimes serves to make symptoms clearer than they would be through simple auditory perception. If you experiment yourself you may discover exercises that are more effective than the ones offered in this collection. You may also sense something of the psychological dynamic of the symptom that provides a basis for conversations with the client.

3. Needs and concerns of the clients.

The state or a particular concern of a client (for example, tiredness, being highly strung, pre-examination stress, presentations, and so on) may make it impossible to take the next intended step in a therapy. Some kind of 'situation report' at the beginning of the sitting serves to clarify the client's current frame of mind, or helps to establish the stage the client has reached in his or her search, testing or practising. To ask 'How are you?' on greeting a client is of no help here, because it is mostly understood to be a meaningless phrase and provokes an analogous response.

The questions should be asked in such a way that it is clear that the direction of the treatment is in the hands of the client: for example, 'What is of importance to you today?', or 'What do you want to do today?', or 'Where do you want to start today?'

In principle, the concerns and needs of the clients always take priority. As treatment progresses and the client becomes increasingly independent this third approach plays a more decisive role in deciding which exercises are chosen.

The contents of a sitting do not, however, become random through looking into the momentary situation of the client. All three approaches need to be taken into account simultaneously, which means that a rigid therapy plan cannot be devised for a particular sitting.

Some requirements for therapists are:

1. From a functional perspective, certainty in their methodology and a corresponding collection of exercises for approaching individual kinds of problems adequately.

What leads to and belongs to this certainty is one's own experiences with exercises and constant 'sticking to' working on the development of one's own voice.

2. On the person-oriented level, composure and inner peace that protect against activism. The therapists must give the clients space and must tolerate any 'empty' space that may occur as a

result in the therapy session. A means of achieving the necessary abilities for this is self-awareness.

Exercise Procedure

Motivation of Clients

As explained in Chapter 2, pp. 27–28, transparency of content of therapy is a basic principle of PVT. This means that it is necessary for the therapist to provide the client with a reason for a particular exercise being chosen, something that is meant to ensure the client's active participation.

The reason for conducting an exercise can be given either before or after an exercise:

1. Providing reasons prior to the exercise.
   This becomes essential in the initial phase of the treatment if clients are offered exercises which they had not expected would be part of voice therapy. This applies to the whole category of work on the body. The first exercise for work on the body generally begins with the client lying down on the ground, which means that it will be necessary to provide the clients with information subsequent to the examination and anamnesis. If the clients are psychologically attuned to work on the body they will be able to dress accordingly.
   With other exercises that fall under different categories and that clients might find odd, it is also sensible to provide information on them in advance.
2. Providing reasons after the exercise.
   Another possibility would be to advise the clients that an explanation for the exercise will be given at a later stage to prevent influencing the clients' perception and experience.

The Subject of 'Demonstrating – Imitating'

PVT seldom resorts to using direct imitation, which means that exercises are rarely demonstrated to clients.

The trained voice of the therapist is very easily used as a criterion by the clients, which means that the clients are easily frustrated if they find that they are not capable of producing the same quality of sound. This leads to their evaluating what is 'right or wrong', preventing them from experimenting with their voices in a non-judgemental way. The idea is to discover their own voices and not to imitate the voice of the therapist.

When, for example, a phonation exercise is conducted in the form of a dialogue, the situation is different. The communicative aspect becomes most important and the risk of the clients' orienting themselves too much with regard to the therapist's voice is reduced. A positive effect of exercises that involve dialogue is that clients are swept along by the therapist and gain the courage to speak more.

Using Experimenting as a Method

The therapist tries to put the clients on the right track to achieving optimal voice function by making suggestions and encouraging them to try out different approaches. This means that the therapist will need to explain to the clients that the exercises are concerned with experimenting with different ways of using the voice before they start. Trying out new behaviour in practice situations is still 'harmless', but can be very revealing. The point at which we 'shy away like a horse in front of a hurdle' is usually where our problems lie (for example, fear of a loud voice).

The decision over what is suitable for transfer into everyday language is left open for the present and remains the decision of the client at a later time. On page 29 we gave the example of a client not wanting to transfer her newly discovered voice into everyday life since she was worried about the adverse effects it would have on her partnership.

Great importance is laid on clients correcting themselves when they experiment with an alternative mode of conduct. The therapist's questions encourage them to do this, for example, 'What could you still change?', or 'What would you still like to change?', or 'Would you like to try it again in a slightly different way?'

Conscious transfer from one vocal behaviour to another where the pathological movement pattern directly opposes the physiological often allows the clients themselves to find out how they can achieve a physiological function without external intervention on the part of the therapist.

'Homework'

The idea of homework is incompatible with PVT since it would imply the clients becoming pupils and the therapists becoming controlling teachers.

Clients are not going to practise at home because a therapist has instructed them to do so. If they do it on the basis of this motivation (obedience) the change in their voices will be short-lived. They will only 'practise' if they strive inwardly to bring about a change in their voices in order to lend expression to a change in their personalities.

An example from work on tonus/posture may serve to make this clear:

You can practise upright posture as a precondition for optimal breathing and vocal output. The relevant back muscles can also be trained. If 'practising posture' for 20 minutes each day is seen as training it will not bring about long-term change. All it does is enable the client to be conscious of a new kind of bodily sensation, although there may also be the positive aspect of having been able to withdraw from everyday stress for a short period of time. A real change in conduct can only occur through an altered state of consciousness since external posture reflects internal posture. Conduct needs to be checked against different situations and in relation to all kinds of people if a decision in favour of a change is to be reached.

The issue of homework, in particular, is one on which therapists have a completely different view. They think that the more a particular process of, for example, relaxing or straightening the sacrum, sternum and back of the neck are practised at home, the higher the likelihood of the treatment being successful.

In some cases of organic vocal disorders (like compensation for the closure of the glottis in cases of partial paralysis of the recurrent nerve) appropriate intensive practice may be advisable. In most cases of functional voice disorders this fixation with practice holds the following dangers:

1. The clients are doing something for their voices but they lack the relation to themselves. They are surprised that no long-term change occurs despite the fact that they have done 'so much'. The treatment sessions and, as the case may be, daily exercise programme take on the character of an 'outlet' through which the clients get rid of the responsibility for their voices.
2. The therapists can detract from their own helplessness with regard to success not having been achieved by placing the 'blame' on the client for not having practised enough: 'Without your regularly practising there is little I can do to help you.' If clients find that this is the situation then they can most delicately extract themselves from it by realising that, 'These exercises are not for me.'

3. The clients cling to the therapists and suck them dry through forever wanting to try out more and more new exercises which might have a better effect – or, indeed, have any effect. Or they just enjoy receiving 'treatment', since, after all, relaxation, breathing and voice exercises are for the most part pleasant and normally do not hurt.

Work on the Personal Level

Reflection

Reflection after the exercises is the direct path (door opener) to the personal level.

Immediately after every exercise an appropriate space of time should be set aside for allowing the exercise to linger in the mind and to reflect upon thoughts and feelings. Conversations in PVT arise as a direct result of practical exercise work and should, as a rule, lead back to practice again, irrespective of whether there are sittings in which conversation dominates.

There are different ways to achieve a reflective state of mind:

1. Spontaneous comments made by clients.
   At the beginning of treatment clients are unlikely to be used to talking about their own thoughts in treatment or instructional situations without being asked to do so. If, however, time to reflect becomes a well established part of the treatment, it becomes more of a habit for clients spontaneously to voice their opinion of the exercise after it has been completed. By doing this they are signalling that the work is important for them on a personal level.
2. Asking the clients questions.
   By asking well aimed questions the therapists can incite the clients to reflect; for example:
   'How did you feel the exercise went?'
   'How did you find your altered voice?'
   To take a step further would be the examination of a concrete reaction to a particular exercise. The following, for example, could be examined:
   whether a client reacts in a similar way in different situations;
   whether a client is aware of why he or she is acting in a particular way;
   how those around the client react to his or her behaviour.

3. Therapists' observations.

   Clients emit numerous verbal and non-verbal signals in the course of exercises that can reveal the effect of an exercise. The more accurate the perception of the therapist is, the more signals they are able to take on board and are able to address. It is important that, when doing so, they describe their observations without interpreting them; for example:

   'I had the feeling that you found the exercise difficult.'

   'I noticed that you became restless when you did this exercise.'

   Or

   'I got the impression that you became very calm.'

The reaction of a client can always mean something different and it is presumptuous to interpret it externally. Falling asleep during a body exercise, for example, may simply be due to tiredness and may not signify rejection. A quiet voice during phonation exercises may sound shy. However, this does not necessarily mean that the client is shy. Maybe he or she is just being cautious?

What counts is not 'This is the way the client is', but, 'What do I perceive?' The speech behaviour of a person has a different effect on different listeners. One person may find somebody's voice arrogant, whereas somebody else may describe the same voice as being distanced or cautious. Therapists should be aware of the subjectivity with which they perceive voices.

Three possibilities can be differentiated from clients' reactions to the exercises:

1. The exercise was pleasant.

   The clients hereby reveal that there is the possibility of their advancing from the point reached or that they have discovered something that was previously missing by doing this (for example, peace, certainty).

2. The exercise was unpleasant.

   The question of why it was unpleasant can be scrutinised (for example, restlessness occurring) or whether there are parallels with similar situations.

3. The exercise did not trigger off a reaction.

   This could mean that the perception of the clients has not yet changed enough or that reflection on their feelings is not (yet) desired by them. The latter is possibly an important guard. What is decisive is that therapists do not exercise 'reflection terror'. It is enough continually to offer reflection as a possibility in order to point to the connection between voice and self. Let us once more emphasise:

Work on a personal level is an offer made to the client. The extent to which they go along with it is up to them.

Reacting to Reflection

We differentiate between two basic ways of reacting:

1. Looking into an individual problem.
   The precondition for this is that the clients clearly present their problem and thereby signal that they wish to enter into a conversation with the therapist. This conversation is conducted taking into consideration the principles of conversation (Rogers, 1965). Through the therapist's listening and accepting, the clients find support in treating their problems. It is essential that the therapist refrains from giving direct advice, but this does not rule out personal points of view.
2. Thematisation through generalisation
   This possibility presents itself when the clients address the subject but are not prepared to see a connection to their personal situation. For example, a client wants to talk about stress at work in general, but not about his or her own stress. The barrier that the client hereby signals is accepted by the therapist. The connection between the reaction to an exercise and the self is apparent, but it is left up to the client as to how far he or she wishes to go along with the clarification process. The therapists are in the position of being able to offer different perspectives or to speak of personal experience with regard to the topic at hand. Going back to our example, by mentioning well known possibilities of coping with stress you can inform or report on how you yourself try to cope with stress.
   This often encourages the clients to participate and often brings the subject round to the clients themselves.
   The basis of all conversations with clients about their problem should be trust in their creativity and ability to solve their problems of their own accord. The task of the therapist is to initiate this process and to accompany and thereby offer clarification and assistance.

The Boundary between PVT and Psychotherapy

Among colleagues and in the training of speech therapists the question often arises as to where the line is to be drawn between PVT and psychotherapy.

It is possible to mark out a boundary on the basis of the fundamentally different tasks of PVT and psychotherapy. Voice therapy is primarily concerned with working on and training the voice in cases of impaired voice function. Particular methods are selected with this task in mind, whereby PVT draws the person as a whole into its work.

In psychotherapy the 'personal level' is the primary area of treatment. Concrete methods, dependent on the relevant psychotherapeutic direction, are available that aim to initiate or accompany psychological processes. Concrete methods exist aimed at initiating or accompanying psychological processes that depend on the relevant psychotherapeutic direction.

In the case of practical voice work, it is difficult clearly to draw a line. Because of the connection between voice and self it is ineffective or even impossible to work on voice function in isolation. Voice therapists will therefore constantly have to grapple with the boundaries of their profession.

There are three main aspects that are relevant in this connection:

1. Being alert to and sensible of the limits signalled by the client and at the same time accepting these limits (compare p. 174).
2. Sensing and accepting the limits of one's own competence or one's personal involvement in a problem of the client.
3. The readiness to be self-aware and supervise therapeutic work.

The following case study offers a clearer picture on how a psychological problem can be touched upon by work on voice function yet will still need to be worked upon outside speech therapy.

Case study

Mrs P. is 54 years old. She is referred to a speech therapist with a voice disorder after having repeatedly had leukoplakias removed. In discussing the anamnesis Mrs P. says that she has had a problem with her voice for almost exactly three years, from the time her son had a fatal motorbike accident.

Because of the concrete temporal connection it appears most likely that the shocking experience caused Mrs P.'s voice disorder. However, in the course of conversations in further sittings Mrs P. gives the impression that she has got over the death of her son.

The work with Mrs P. is difficult to arrange. When it comes to exercises intended for regulating tension, on the one hand she signals great willingness, while on the other she reacts with a shortness of breath and obvious fear. This increasingly affects her therapy. She explains that she likes coming for treatment and feels comfortable but is 'somehow' at the same time also scared of it. Through discussion the attempt is made to understand this contradiction. In the process the subject of the different gender of therapist and patient crops up. It is only after several sittings that she reveals that it takes a lot of effort for her to lie down on the exercise mat. She rejects the offer to refrain from this kind of exercise, giving the reason that 'the treatment does me good and somehow the exercises are important for me'.

After she has been in therapy for a longer period of time, during which a further decortication of her vocal fold takes place, Mrs P. one day relates an awful experience. She remembers having been sexually abused by her much older brother-in-law at the age of 13.

Although she has seen this brother-in-law time and time again over the years, it was only when she suffered the strong emotional shock of her son's funeral that she had her first inkling of what had happened. The patient describes that on meeting at the occasion of the funeral, she only knew: 'He shouldn't be here!'

The intensive work on the body that was carried out within the framework of the therapy was a constant stirring-up of this memory. Further conversations suggest that Mrs P. sees many of her current problems and behavioural patterns in the context of her terrible experiences as a child.

This is the point of demarcation of PVT and psychotherapy.

It is made clear to the patient that in order to deal with the problems resulting from her early traumatic experience the competence of a psychotherapist is required and that it is not possible for her to work on them within the context of voice therapy.

13

Personal Aspects of Specific Disorders

Here we discuss the use of PVT in the case of specific disorders with which voice therapists are often confronted.

The aim is to clarify what extra significance, beyond work on a functional level, the inclusion of the personal aspect has.

Organic Voice Disorders

Organic voice disorders are those related to changes of voice sound caused by a pathological change to the larynx or vocal tract. In speech therapeutic practice this includes, in particular, laryngeal paralysis and partial excision of the larynx, as well as oedemas, polyps and vocal fold nodules.

Laryngectomy, the complete removal of the larynx, will not be discussed in this book. Although loss of voice is, in a further sense, also a voice disorder, the particular problems of this disorder require a specific therapeutic procedure.

The Functional Side of Organic Voice Disorders

If organic changes to the vocal folds occur it is essential that an exact differential diagnosis examination by an ENT specialist is undertaken. This will decide whether medical measures will be necessary for the voice disorder or whether voice therapy is indicated. In the case of unclear diagnoses or of therapy that is stagnating, voice therapists should not be reluctant to suggest that the patients have a further examination.

The following questions are of fundamental significance for the therapeutic procedure and the course of treatment since they shed light on what, if anything, can be done from the organic perspective of voice function.

Are nodules soft or already hardened?

In the case of a Reinke-oedema, is operative removal indicated?

Is an instance of paralysis of the vocal fold in middle position actually a consequence of a phonatory arrest?

Where hoarseness has existed since childhood, is it possible to rule out a sulcus glottidis?, and so on.

As already explained (in Part II), vocal fold vibration and therefore the voice result from an interplay of glottal resistance and subglottal breath pressure. The component glottal resistance which consists of position, tension and mass of the vocal folds may be affected in different ways in the case of voice disorders.

For example, laryngoparalysis may, depending on the position and tension of the paralysed vocal fold, mean that the glottis is prevented from closing. This causes the valve function to be suspended or to be considerably restricted, the periodic interruption of the air flow is no longer possible. In spite of this, in order to cause the vocal folds to vibrate, the amount of breath pressure is built up, but this is exuded unused. The voice sounds extremely aspirated.

In the case of a Reinke-oedema the space between the mucosa and muscle tissue is filled with liquid. This causes the entire mass of the vocal fold to increase, which in turn requires an increase in breath pressure. The vibratory function of vocal fold mucosa is no longer possible. The vocal fold 'swings' inertly and awkwardly, the voice sounds deep, monotonous and, usually, choked.

With regard to physiological voice production, organic changes to vocal folds primarily represent mechanical impairments of the vibration process. The aim of voice therapy is to compensate for these impairments as effectively as possible.

The aetiology of many organic changes to the vocal folds is not clear. Often a vocal malfunction is taken as the cause. On the other hand, organic voice disorders usually result in erroneous compensation. What therefore needs to be treated in voice therapy is the cause of malfunction as well as the unfavourable compensation attempts by the patients.

It is therefore vital to be in possession of exact knowledge of the voice function and to carry out carefully aimed exercises for the treatment of organic voice disorders.

This becomes clear if we look at, for example, a partial paralysis of the recurrent nerve. In order to achieve a new voice function, voice therapist and patient need to overcome the following problems: on the one hand it makes sense to activate the mobile vocal fold in such a way that it oscillates beyond the middle line, rests against the paralysed vocal fold and results in the closure of the glottis. When this happens the tension in the healthy vocal fold may only increase to a degree where oscillation is maintained. The aim is to achieve the greatest possible amplitude, which requires looseness and elasticity. On the other hand, increased activity is necessary in order for the vocal folds to come closer together.

This, in turn, requires a very different kinaesthetic perception on the part of the patient involved. Heightened awareness is therefore just as important in the case of organic voice disorders as it is for functional voice disorders.

Voice therapists need to have a good ear, good power of observation and different methods to choose from in order to be able to demonstrate to their patients how impeded voice function can be compensated for as economically as possible.

Personal and Organic Voice Disorders

Two basic aspects can be differentiated on the personal side of organic voice disorders:

personal components of the cause;

consequences for the affected person.

1. Personal components of the cause.

   If one goes on the assumption that organic voice disorders are mostly caused by vocal malfunctions (compare Wirth, 1995) then it follows that what causes the malfunction needs to be treated. This embraces the personal level.

   Of course, the kind of organic disorder at hand must be distinguished. In the case of a postoperative partial paralysis of the recurrent nerve, for example, to ask the question found in Chapter 2, pp. 15–16, 'understanding what the voice wants to say', would be completely inappropriate. But in the case of a Reinke-oedema that may be viewed as an organic manifestation of increased hyper-functionality, this question is very important. The cause of the Reinke-oedema does not ultimately lie in the hyper-functional use of the voice, but in the conditions that led to its hyper-functionality in the first place. This also applies to vocal fold polyps and, to a certain extent, to vocal fold nodules. It is therefore essential to incorporate the whole person into the treatment.

2. Consequences of organic voice disorders for the person.

   An important aspect in the treatment of organic voice disorders is consequences arising for the people concerned due to their changed voice function.

The verbatim quote of a patient who has an idiopathic partial paralysis of the recurrent nerve in an intermediary position is intended to clarify this:

> 'I used to be the leading dog, now I don't even belong to the herd any more.' The patient was an executive of a furniture company. Now he is out of work following a six-month illness. 'When I wake up in the morning and hear myself barking, I could tear my hair out in anger.' And further: 'What is even worse than my awful voice is the fact that I cannot do anything about it.'

The organic voice disorder of the patient confronts him with 'personal' issues, such as anger, helplessness and despair.

Emotional expression such as laughing, crying, sighing, groaning, moaning, wailing, shouting for joy are vocal expressions. In the case of some organic voice disorders these are altered considerably or no longer possible.

The finer nuances in the intonation of the voice do not take place. Differences in voice production such as tenderness, determination, questioning, scepticism, encouragement, and so on, are ironed out.

To quote a patient: *'Whether I say good morning to my wife or have an argument with her, everything sounds the same.'*

Depending on how the voice disorder manifests itself, words or stresses in sentences that are determined by vocal emphasis are no longer produced in the correct way. This means that the semantic function of the voice is affected. The patient's power of expression is clearly limited and one aim of voice therapy can be to improve non-verbality, that is, the non-vocal power of expression. How well patients are able to do this automatically directs their attention to their self as a person.

The personal structure of a patient is touched upon when treating organic dysphonias when work is done on tonus, breathing, phonation and articulation. The following examples serve to clarify this point:

If it is necessary to increase or decrease tension of a disturbed voice in order to compensate economically, we cannot ignore the overall tonus of the patient. It may already have tended towards being hyper- or hypotonic prior to the illness and may have been exacerbated due to the current illness.

If it is necessary to balance the primary voice function of the disturbed voice through the creation of maximum space in the jaw, this leads to an improvement in resonance, as is the case with clients who have functional voice disorders; the theme of 'opening oneself' can be touched upon.

It can be concluded from this that when organic voice disorders arise voice therapists should not be fixated on the relevant organ either. They are called upon to view a being as an entity, as a whole that needs to be taken into consideration during treatment.

Disorders of Children's Voices

As with all functional and organic voice disorders, with children's voice disorders it is vital that an examination be done by an ear, nose and throat specialist. The specialist must rule out organic, hormonal and, most importantly, audiogenic causes.

A search for concepts relating to the treatment of children's voice disorders in specialised literature will reveal that recent publications refer to a dual-track approach. Apart from working directly with the child, particular importance is placed on consulting parents. It appears that a voice disorder going beyond mere malfunction is given greater weight in therapeutic processes for the treatment of children's voice disorders than for adults'.

Working with Children

A distinction can be drawn between the direct and indirect influence of symptoms in voice therapy for children with vocal disturbances. Influencing directly may be sensible in the case of the younger patients when it comes to work on achieving the contrast of 'loose' and 'tight'. This applies both to individual muscle areas and to body tension as a whole, as well as to voice function directly. It goes without saying that this must be done in a playful manner (Eberle, 1977a).

An indirect effect on the symptom, on the voice disorder, is achieved by the therapist's conduct towards the child. The therapist must show determination to understand and accept the child unconditionally. No expectations with regard to voice function should be formulated. All exercises should be treated like a game; one that not only has an aim, but should also be made as enjoyable as possible. There should be no prohibitions, such as, for example, 'You're not allowed to shout!'; and support should be offered, for example, 'I'll show you how you can shout even louder!'

Working with Parents

The primary aim of working with parents is to take the burden off them and to alleviate the fears and pressure they feel on account of their child having a voice disorder. This applies in particular to vocal nodules that are often, even if only subconsciously, associated with malignancy.

In addition to considering the voice disorder from a functional point of view, that is, to explaining the anatomical and physiological context, parents should be encouraged to consider from a person-oriented perspective their child's voice or voice disorder.

The purpose is not to make the parents feel guilty or to put the blame for the child's voice disorder on them, but rather to pose questions in the form of hypotheses that lead to a better understanding of the child and reveal possible reasons for the symptom. The endeavour to 'understand what the voice wants to say' also applies to the voice or voice disorder of the child.

Taking a personal look at the child's disturbed voice leads to questions such as:

What pressure is the child under?
What role does he or she play in the family?
What is his or her position in playgroup or in school?
How does he or she gain attention and make him- or herself heard?
Is the child good at asserting him- or herself or is he or she easily dominated?
How much space does the living environment offer for playing games?
Is there a daily routine to the child's life?
Does the child have a busy schedule of ballet, riding, swimming, and so on that allows little time for dreaming or lazing about?
In which situations is the child required to speak?
Do the conversation partners have time to listen?
How frequently are the television and video recorder on, even if only in the background?

The pressure that the child might feel under may find an outlet via the valve of the voice. Whether the child reacts vocally may also depend on the type of child he or she is.

Children who are very lively and expressive by nature often express themselves verbally and vocally while they are playing: the purring lorry engine, the screeching wheels, the roaring lion, and so on.

Howling, shrieking, groaning, squeaking and bawling, for example, are means used on various occasions to lend expression to the respective situations.

Diversity of expression and pleasure of expression shown by a child, within the context of the child's voice disorder, should not be evaluated as a misuse of voice.

It is important to encourage this and the child's expressing itself non-verbally or in non-vocal ways. This is the only way that the child will experience the treatment as something exonerating and enriching and not as a restriction or criticism aimed at the child.

Disorders of the Singing Voice

When talking about the use of the singing voice, we would like to make a distinction between people who sing (from laymen to committed choir singers) and singers (professionals).

Voice therapists come across both groups in their practice, which means that they are confronted with the question of the possibilities and limits of voice therapy.

Before we say anything about the personal aspect of singing, we would like briefly to explain the functional particularities of the singing voice. Our explanation will confine itself to the essential difference of the speaking voice in the sub-categories: breathing and the function of diaphragm; primary voice function and secondary voice function.

The Singing Voice as a Special Function

1. Breathing and the function of the diaphragm.
   In the case of breathing that accompanies singing, the time ratio of inhalation and exhalation is altered in terms of pause and speaking breath (compare Chapter 5) from 1 : 10 to 1 : 50 (Wirth, 1995). This is mainly due to the increased function of the diaphragmatic support, which minimises the pressure of breath. Whereas while breathing during speech the division of the speech phrases should mirror the breathing rhythm, the literature shows that the way breathing is proportioned while singing can be very different. Sometimes very long phrases, the

sense or effect of which would be ruined if they were interrupted by breathing, are required.

Furthermore, singing coloraturas or sounds with vibrato require the greatest possible flexibility and elasticity of the diaphragm. The rapid changes of pitch in vibrato, five to seven times per second (Wirth, 1995) need to be responded to with the smallest possible changes to the pressure of breath.

We have already mentioned that the diaphragm sinks along with a low position of the larynx. This means that the abdominal-pelvic region and the muscles of the pelvic floor need to be relaxed, which has a twofold effect on resonance: first, the direct resonance space of the vocal tract is enlarged through the low position of the larynx; second, body resonance benefits from the relaxed state.

2. Primary voice function.

The modulation span, that is, the tonal range when speaking, moves around the middle speaking pitch and covers a little more than one octave. While singing, the voice range is, in particular, increased upwards and, in the case of a trained voice, can cover more than three octaves. This requires enormous elasticity and flexibility of the laryngeal musculature, which determines the length and tension of the vocal folds and therefore the move from one register to another must occur in a flowing manner without interruptions.

Vocal fold initiation that, from a physiological point of view, is deemed firm when speaking is perceptibly soft when singing.

The crescendo (*messa di voce*) is a further function that is of great importance for singing yet does not occur in the speaking voice. The volume is changed while the note sung remains at the same pitch. This requires a different kind of fine-tuning of the laryngeal muscles, since pitch normally increases as the volume increases.

3. Secondary voice function.

Secondary voice function refers to the direct resonatory formation of a tone in the vocal tract, which is completed by head and body resonance. Resonance and capacity result from richness in the upper partials. These are in turn determined by a pronounced structure of singing formants. Even though resonance and capacity are important for the speaking voice, these vocal achievements are indispensable for singing. They should not be confused with volume.

Much more effort is required from the singer to achieve balanced vowels than from the speaker. This concerns the forming of vowels in such a way that the difference in tone between those that are light ('e', 'i') and those that are dark ('o', 'u') is balanced out. If, for example, the full vocal vowel 'a' is sung without control in a low pitch, it will sound very chesty and 'heavy' and even the intonation (hitting the required pitch) will be too low. The same vowel 'a' becomes more slight and lighter if it is sung with less vibrating mass of the vocal folds and admixture of head resonance.

Amateur Singers in Voice-therapeutic Treatment

Singing may not be a vital function but it can be an expression of the joy of living and contentedness, as well as other feelings. This means that singing has a valve function in a personal sense.

At the same time, singing is an activity that can have a marked effect on its listeners since it is able to please, placate, animate, and so on.

The pedagogic effect of singing is evident in playgroups and primary schools. This is why the singing voice has professional significance for educators and teachers.

After all, singing and song stand high on the agenda of many people when they plan their leisure activities. In clubs and choirs people sing so that they can both fulfil a musical interest and experience contact and social interaction with others.

Work on the impaired singing voice within the context of voice therapy is always necessary and justified when the disorder prevents the person affected from performing his or her professional role, or when the incorrect use of the singing voice so influences the speaking voice that on account of this there is a danger of the speaking voice itself becoming impaired.

There is a diagnostic aspect to working with people who sing, one that involves examining their song pattern for non-physiological processes. There is a therapeutic part to it, which lies in acquiring the basic functions of singing. These are identical to those of the speaking voice. So it is not special exercises for the singing voice that we are concerned with, but rather the building of a bridge between the use of the speaking voice and the singing voice. The voice therapist's task lies in getting the 'instrument, voice' to sound harmonious again. The instructions on virtuoso playing of this instrument then fall into the area of singing pedagogics.

Taking Care of the Voice

Much more attention is paid to the quality of a person's voice when singing than when speaking. Form and content of what is vocally expressed have equal importance, and indeed form may be given even greater importance.

Given this, it is understandable that many clients who sing ask for 'tips'.

As far as cautionary measures that can be taken to ensure that the voice stays healthy are concerned, we can return to the picture of the string instrument. The violinist wraps his instrument in a soft cloth before placing it in its case. By doing this he protects it from getting scratched and it also helps to prevent damage occurring through climatic change.

Singers in particular can relate to this pictorial comparison from the field of instrumental music. Transferring the image of a musician looking after and treating his or her instrument carefully to the way we treat the instrument, voice, means paying attention to the following points:

Avoid clearing your throat. If you are forced to cough, then attempt to deal with it by humming or fluttering your lips.

Avoid extremely cold or hot food and drinks. These have a detrimental effect on blood flow in the mucosal covering.

Increase the body's defences through a generally healthy lifestyle: eat a well balanced diet, and avoid stress.

Avoid dryness: if necessary, turn up the humidifier and drink plenty of non-alcoholic liquids.

Avoid speaking when the level of background noise is very high.

Ensure that there is sufficient body warmth (foot bath) when you have a cold. Take inhalations.

Of the Fortune and Misfortune of Professional Singers

In order optimally to master the functions described on pp. 183–185 that produce a good singing voice, a number of preconditions have to be satisfied. The first is, without doubt, intensive training. The second is a particular disposition, that is, organic conditions that enable one to keep up with the particular effort required for the art of singing.

Finally, 'beautiful' singing requires a certain amount of talent.

As a rule, all singers satisfy these preconditions. They are in the fortunate position of being able to use their voices like a tuneful instrument, with which they can convey feeling and content. They can express themselves in a way surpassing the 'normal' level, which is why the effect they can achieve is often special. The listener is moved, touched, enraptured, and so on.

When singers use their voices they need to perform a feat. On the one hand, they need to train their voices and work hard on them and, on the other, they need to produce effortlessness by being physically and psychologically relaxed. Technical voice perfection (function) and 'being at one with oneself' (personality) need to complement one another. This is what may also turn the fortune mentioned above into misfortune. The organ that is capable of expressing strong emotion is not allowed to react to feelings of its own that may interfere with this expression.

Because a singer's voice is his or her instrument, it must always be fully functional. Concert dates are often booked months in advance and do not make allowances for actual state of health on the day of performance. The listeners have paid their entrance fee and expect to experience high quality in return. The expectations of the listeners are often based on their personal listening experience, which is subject to increased technicalisation (CD).

Finally, the pressure of competition in the artistic market is huge. Singers are regarded as 'goods' that are bought. The smallest defects or growing older lead to a fall in demand.

It becomes clear what kind of pressure the voices of singers are under and how their valuation affects their performance.

Professional Singers in Voice Therapy

As a rule, voice therapists are not singing teachers. This frequently leads to their being reluctant to treat those who are having problems with their singing voice, or even professional singers. They feel that they do not possess the necessary competence as therapists when compared to specialists, or they feel that they are under a certain amount of pressure as far as their own voices are concerned. The question is, what do voice therapists have to 'offer' singers?

Case study

A soprano goes into treatment after a nose, ear and throat specialist has ascertained that she is starting to get nodules on her vocal folds. The symptoms, which may be hardly noticeable in her voice, are to be recorded by a sonogram at the beginning of the treatment, so that the course of treatment can be documented.

When her vocal range is measured, her competence as a singer is evident. With great precision she describes how she produces tones, shows her awareness of where changes in register take place and, despite the findings, projects a wonderful lightness. From this the therapist draws the conclusion that the voice disorder can hardly stem from her using a wrong technique and voices his opinion that he suspects that the problems lie 'elsewhere'. The singer shows relief and says that she feels understood.

This is a marvellous result from a sitting aimed at obtaining a diagnosis that merely ended with a short conversation. The important signals for the soprano singer are that her singing capabilities are not disputed and that she receives the recognition that she is a person as well as a singer.

The following treatment comprises merely concentrated work on the body in conjunction with conversations.

The main content of these conversations are issues such as:

What function/significance does singing have for me?

How do I deal with my speaking voice, particularly in confrontations?

What can I express in song that I cannot express in spoken words?

What would the rest of my life be like if I could not sing in concerts again?

What qualities do I possess apart from the ability to sing?

Which roles suit me; which ones do I dislike?

Which conductors do I dislike working with?

There are far-reaching changes that occur in the client. She restricts the amount of concerts she gives and only accepts engagements that she really enjoys. She dedicates herself to something completely new and starts studying medicine. Finally she no longer 'preserves' her voice when arguing with others. The nodules disappear after several weeks.

This example clarifies two points:

1. The fundamental stance of PVT, 'understanding what the voice (the person) wants to say', also applies to singers, if not more so. What singers often experience when in communication with others is that interest shown in them is directed at their art rather

than at themselves as a human beings. In voice therapy they can and should have a different experience.

2. A change in voice can only be brought about through changes in attitude and behaviour. This also applies to 'voice professionals'.

14
Goals of PVT

What to Expect from Voice Therapy

The general goal of voice therapy is based on the expectation that, even from different directions, a successful course of voice therapy can always be proposed.

1. The expectations of the doctor.
   The doctor prescribes 'voice exercise treatment', thereby assigning a voice therapist. Like prescribing medication, the doctor expects this to have long-term effects. Laryngoscopic or stroboscopic examinations allow him or her to control the success of this treatment.
2. The expectations of the National Health Service or health insurance company.
   As the bearer of the cost of voice therapy, the National Health Service or health insurance company has the right to expect that the measures financed by it are successful.
3. The expectations of the clients.
   Clients are referred by the doctor, placing their trust in the doctor that the prescribed treatment will bring about the cure of their complaint.
4. The expectations of the therapist.
   Therapists themselves expect their efforts to yield success. They have learnt their 'trade' and know the effectiveness of the methods they use.

All these expectations are united in their goal of ensuring that treatment leads to an unimpeded and resilient voice. This is what the voice therapist is required to achieve.

Consequences for the Procedural Method

It is understandable that great pressure to perform may arise from the demands mentioned above. This pressure often puts voice therapists on a track that is purely functional. Because they know what the outcome of a particular exercise or method is, they are tempted by what is functionally possible. What worked for client A must have exactly the same effect for client B. In their endeavour to achieve an optimal voice function as quickly as possible, the reasons that caused the function to be disturbed in the first place become secondary or are ignored.

The described effort in ensuring a perfect voice function reflects the way voice disorders are understood: a disturbed function is to be un-disturbed. In the process, personal obstruction is frequently overlooked.

Understanding and Aims of Voice Therapy within PVT

PVT would like to encourage a different understanding of voice disorders. Abresch (1988) correctly describes them as 'the soundtrack of crisis'. It is not an isolated function that is disturbed, but the disturbed function is an expression of 'disorder' in the whole person. The goal of a voice therapy must attune itself to this fact. Accordingly, the methodological procedure in PVT is different and more extensive: the personal level is part of the therapy.

With the setting of a different goal the 'success' of a voice therapy is, at the same time, defined anew (compare Chapter 2, pp. 30–31). The categorical aims of PVT and the general goals of therapy are represented in Figure 14.1.

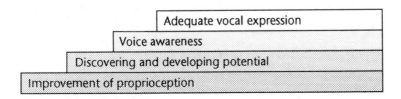

Figure 14.1

A generally improved awareness of the voice leads to discovering and developing one's own potential. An improved awareness of the possibilities and limits of the voice in different situations is connected with this. The voice awareness that is achieved leads to greater general awareness. Sometimes the voice already 'knows' at a very early stage and becomes a reliable indicator of factors that burden. The expectations with regard to the 'performance' – ability of the voice – become relative and the acceptance of voice symptoms becomes greater. This altered way of dealing with the symptoms and one's own state of health means that the symptom itself loses its meaning and can therefore disappear.

The result is adequate, self-aware vocal expression.

Bibliography

Abresch, J. 1988. 'Stimmstörungen als Krisenvertonung' in *Integrative Therapie* 1/88: 40–62.

Alexander, F.M. 1985. *The Use of the Self.* London. Gollancz.

Alexander, G. 1992. *Eutonie.* Munich. Kösel.

Barth, V. 1982. *Die Lumpenstroboskopie.* Knittlingen. Wolf.

Bay, E. 1991. 'Individualpsychologische Therapie' in Kraiker and Peter (eds), 1991.

Berne, E. 1982. *Games People Play.* London. Penguin.

Biesalski, P. and Frank, F. (eds). 1991. *Phoniatrie.* Stuttgart. Thieme.

Böhme, G. 1980. *Therapie der Sprach-, Sprech- und Stimmstörungen.* Stuttgart. Fischer.

Brand, U. 1992. *Eutonie, natürliche Spannkraft.* Munich. Gräfe und Unzer.

Brügge, W. and Mohs, K. 1994. *Therapie funktioneller Stimmstörungen.* Munich. Reinhardt.

Buchs-Quante, U. 1994. 'Wege zur Singstimme' in *LOGOS Interdisziplinär* 3/94: 206–13.

Cardas, E. 1989. *Atmen, Lebenskraft befreien.* Munich. Gräfe und Unzer.

Clausen-Söhngen, M. et al. 1988. 'Logopädische Diagnostik und Therapie bei Stimmstörungen'. Aachen. Unpublished manuscript.

Coblenzer, H. 1987. *Erfolgreich Sprechen.* Vienna. ÖBV.

Coblenzer, H. and Muhar, F. 1976. *Atem und Stimme.* Vienna. ÖBV, 1993 edition.

Dinkelacker, R. 1987. 'Übungen für die Sprechstimme'. Stuttgart. Unpublished manuscript.

Draayer, H. 1984. *Finde dich selbst durch Meditation.* Munich. Kösel.

Dürckheim, K. 1985. *The Way of Transformation.* London. Allen & Unwin.

Eberle, A. 1977a. 'Kindliche Dysphonien – Ein Therapiekonzept'. Address delivered at the annual meeting of the ZVL. May 1977.

Eberle, A. 1977b. 'Rahmenplan für die Behandlung von Stimmstörungen'. Unpublished manuscript.

Eberle, A. 1979. 'Mutationsstimmstörungen als Identifikationsproblem – Ein Therapiekonzept' in *Sprache-Stimme-Gehör* 3/79.

Feldenkrais, M. 1980. *Awareness through movement.* London. Penguin.

Franke, U. 1991. *Logopädisches Handlexikon.* Munich. Reinhardt.

Freidrich, G. and Bigenzahn, W. 1995. *Phonatrie*. Bern. Huber.

Fröschels, E. 1940. 'Die Wesenseinheit der Kau- und Artikulations-bewegungen' in *Klinische Wochenschrift* 64.

Gelb, M. 1994. *Body Learning*. London. Aurum.

Grohnfeld, M. (ed.). 1994. *Handbuch der Sprachtherapie / Band 7: Stimmstörungen*. Spiess, Berlin. Ed. Marhold im Wiss.-Verl.

Gundermann, H. 1994. 'Stimmstörungen – Fragen und Gedanken zur Prävention' in *LOGOS Interdisziplinär* 3/94: 167–9.

Habermann, G. 1978. *Stimme und Sprache*. Stuttgart. Thieme.

Husler, F. and Rodd-Marling, Y. 1976. *Singing. The Physical Nature of the Vocal Organ*. London. Hutchinson.

Jung, C. G. 1990. *Mensch und Kultur, Grundwerk Bd. 9*. Olten and Freiburg. Walter.

Kia, R. A. 1991. *Stimme – Spiegel meines Selbst*. Braunschweig. Aurum.

Kjellrup, M. 1993. *Bewußt mit dem Körper leben*. Munich. Ehrenwirth.

Kraiker, C. and Peter, B (eds). 1991. *Psychotherapieführer*. Munich. Beck.

Kriz, J. 1991. *Grundkonzepte der Psychotherapie*. Weinheim. Psychologie Verlags Union.

Kriz, J. 1994. 'Können LogopädInnen psychotherapeutisch arbeiten?' in *LOGOS Interdisziplinär* 2/94: 132–8.

Madelung, E. 1987. *Das Paradox der Selbstwahrnehmung*. Address delivered to the TU Munich, 10 June.

Methling, C., Schaible, A., Westphal, B. and Zaschka, B. 1994. 'Zu Wirkungen und Wirkfaktoren logopädischer Stimmtherapie'. Cologne. Unpublished paper at the Lehranstalt für Logopädie.

Middendorf, I. 1991. *Der erfahrbare Atem*. Paderborn, Jungfermann.

Perls, F. 1987. *Das Ich, der Hunger und die Agression*. Stuttgart. Klett-Cotta.

Rogers, C. R. 1965. *Client-Centered Therapy*. Boston. Houghton Mifflin.

Rohmert, W. (ed.). 1991. *Grundzüge des funktionalen Stimmtrainings*. Cologne. Schmidt.

Ruhl, H. and Strauch, T. 1992. 'Logopädische Diagnostik und Therapie bei Stimmstörungen'. Cologne. Unpublished manuscript.

Satir, V. 1993. *Selbstwert und Kommunikation*. Munich. Pfeiffer.

Schulz von Thun, F. 1992. *Miteinander Reden 1*. Reinbek. Rowohlt.

Simonton, O. C., Matthews-Simonton, S. and Creighton, J. L. 1980. *Getting Well Again*. London. Bantam.

Stengel, I. 1992. 'Personale Stimmtherapie'. Address delivered at the annual meeting of the DBL, Berchtesgaden.

Stengel, I. 1994. 'Person-Centred Voice Therapy'. Address delivered at the second CPLOL-LCSTL European Congress, Antwerp.

Triebel-Thome, A. 1993. *Feldenkrais: Bewegung – ein Weg zum Selbst.* Munich. Gräfe und Unzer.

Wirth, G. 1995. *Stimmstörungen.* Cologne. DAV.

Index

Compiled by Sue Carlton

abdomen-flanks breathing 39–40
abdominal muscles 18
Abresch, J. 191
aggression 113, 128
aikido 24
air dosage 18, 48
alcohol 49
Alexander, Gerda 20, 60
Alexander technique 20, 60
alveolars 52
anamnesis 12–13, 15–16
apportioning of texts 112, 114–15
articulation 36, 52–4
  and aims of therapy 166
  and breathing 154
  consciousness of 154, 155, 156
  exercises 151–7
  and intention 154, 155, 156
  as means of expression 53–4
  releasing tension 92, 93, 95
  valve function 41
articulatory organs 41, 50, 52–3, 54

back muscles 76, 77, 80
Bay, E. 27
Behrend, 3–4
Berne, E. 27
blockages 76, 78, 88
body tension *see* tonus
body vibration 126, 130, 131
body work 20–5, 166
  bodily self-perception (proprio-
    ception) 20, 21–2, 23, 65, 130,
    158
'Breath Rhythm Timed Phonation'
  19, 35, 42, 108–15
breathing 3, 18, 36, 38–43
  and aims of therapy 166
  and centring 24
  during speech 40–3
  exercises 103–19
  and intention 111
  and posture 82
  quiet/calm 38–40, 43, 70, 104–5
  rhythm of 19–20, 40, 42, 129, 130
  and singing 183–4

breathing-voice-articulation,
  unitary function of 154, 157

Cardas, Elena 60
centring 24–5, 70, 86, 89–90, 93, 95
chewing, and speaking 53–4, 127–8
children
  encouraging expression 183
  voice disorders 181–3
  working with parents of 182–3
  working with 181–2
clients
  goals 17
  imagination 12
  interpreting reactions 173
  involvement in process 17, 28,
    168
  motivation 169
  perception of voice disorder 13
  understanding therapy process
    11–12, 16, 18, 19, 20, 27–8
  see also therapist
Coblenzer, H. 19, 35, 41, 42, 60,
  108–15
concentrative body work 20–5
'congruent' reaction 4
consonants, formation of 154, 156–7
controlled conversations 159–60
controlled speaking situations 159
cork, in mouth 155
coughing 49
countertension, consciousness of
  116–17
crescendo 184
crying 94

deep breathing 21, 40
diaphragm 18, 38–9, 49, 90, 108,
  110
  and centring 24
  flexible 40, 149–50
  and posture 107
  and singing 183–4
diaphragmatic suspension 86, 88
Dinkelacker, Ruth 60
directional sounding of tones 131–2

dosage 18, 48
Draayer, Hetty 20, 60
drinking exercise 123

Eberle, Almuth 27, 60, 165, 181
'elastic breathhold' 42, 116, 118, 119
'elastic tension' 24
emotional expression 94, 180
ENT specialists 177, 181, 187
Eutonie 20, 60
eutonus 20, 24, 65, 130
exercises
    abdominal-pelvic region 85–90
    area of articulation and
        phonation 96–102
    articulation 151–7
    body resonance 129–38
    Breath Rhythm Timed
        Phonation 108–15
    conducting 167–76
    division of 60–1
    dynamics of voice 145–50
    expansion of breathing areas
        106–7
    functional level of 61
    independent work 59, 61
    inspiratory countertension
        (support) 116–19
    personal level of 61–2, 172–6
    physiological speaking voice
        register 125–8
    position of sound, vowels and
        syllables 139–44
    posture 79–84
    regulation of tonus 65–74
    resonance space in vocal tract
        122–4, 132
    rhythm of breath 104–5
    selecting 167–9
    shoulder and neck muscles 91–5
    singing voice 185
    sources of 59–60
    spinal column 75–8
    transfer 158–60
    see also Person-Oriented Voice
        Therapy (PVT)
experimentation, as method 170
expiration 39, 40

face 96–7
    caressing with hands 96, 98, 123,
        125, 133, 152
    using stick 96, 125

fairy tales 159
Feldenkrais method 20, 60
frontal position of sound 19
Fröschels, E. 53
'functional voice training' 18

gamma nervous system 23–4
glottal resistance 45–6, 178
Gundermann, H. 3

Habermann, G. 44
hearing, bone conduction 23
hoarseness 178
holding 18
'homework' 170–2
humming 125–6
    and chewing 127

imagination, as agent of change 22
inspiration 38–9, 40
inspiratory countertension
        (support) 42–3, 116–19
    see also support
intention 36, 42–3, 108–9, 110–11
    and articulation 154, 155, 156
    awareness of 112
    and body tension 55–6
intercostal muscles 38, 107
intonation, and organic voice
        disorders 180

jaw, releasing tension 123–4, 133
Jung, C.G. 31

Kriz, J. 21

language, communicating
        sentiment 148
laryngectomy 177
larynx 3, 41, 82
    paralysis of 177, 178
    straightening-out of 86, 88
    tension in 20, 53, 92
    and vowel formation 49–50
    see also vocal folds
'letting off steam' 160
lips 52
lordosis 76

Madelung, E. 20, 21–2
massage 73–4, 99
Middendorf, Ilse 20, 60

modulation 147–8
  span 184
monotony 148
mouth, resonance space 123–4
Muhar, F. 19, 35, 41, 42, 108–15
mumbling 157

nasal sounds 52
newspaper texts 159
nicotine 49

organic dysphoniae 18, 180
  see also voice disorders

palate 52
pausing 112, 115, 160
pelvis
  rotating 87–8
  sounding into 118–19
perfect voice, concept of 4
Perls, F. 54
Person-Oriented Voice Therapy
    (PVT) 7, 8–31
  body awareness 60, 68, 72
  and changing behaviour 9–10
  demonstration and imitation
    169–70
  diagnosis 12–15
  ending treatment 30
  expectations of 190–1
  experimenting 170
  functional level 18
  goals 11, 17, 190–2
  and 'homework' 170–2
  needs of client 11–12
  and organic voice disorders
    177–9, 180–1
  person to voice function 11–12
  personal level 19–20
  procedure 11–12, 18–20
  and psychotherapy 9–10, 175–8
  questions asked 14–15
  role of therapist 25–8
  and self 8–12
  self-reflection 13–14
  and singers 188
  structure of 165–6
  and transfer 28–30
  voice awareness 30–1, 191–2
  voice function to the Self 8–10
  and work on body 20–5, 166
  see also body work; exercises;
    proprioception; transactional
    analysis; voice therapy

'personare' 3–4
phonation (voice production) 36,
    44–51
  and aims of therapy 166
  exercises 121–50
  releasing tension 92, 93, 95
phonatory arrest 178
pictorial descriptions 159
pitch 47–8
  personal 125–6
poems 159
posture 29, 56, 76, 77, 107
  exercises 79–84
primary voice function 184
proprioception (bodily self-
    perception) 20, 21–2, 23, 65,
    94, 130, 158
prose, lyrical 159
'psychogenic aphonia' 15–16
psychotonus 24

reading aloud 114–15
recurrent nerve, paralysis of 178,
    179, 180
reflection 172–4
  reacting to 174
reflex breath completion 41–2, 110
  perceiving 108–9
  and relaxation 41
  and words and phrases 112
Reinke-oedema 178, 179
relaxation, practising 110–11
resonance 48, 49–51, 69, 97
  body 107, 118, 129–32, 184
  and sentences 137–8, 145
  space 122–4, 146, 152, 184
  and syllables 133–4, 135
  and words 135–6, 145
respiration *see* breathing
Rogers, C.R. 174
Rohmert, W. 18

sacrum, sensitising 85–6
Satir, V. 4
secondary voice function 184–5
self-perception *see* proprioception
self-reflection 13–14
shallow breathing 39
shoulders 95
singing
  amateur singers 185
  care of voice 186
  consonants 154

singing continued
   and exercises 185
   modulation span 184
   professional singers 186–9
   as special function 183–5
   and voice disorders 183–9
   volume 184
   and vowels 152
sinus exercise 99–100
Socrates 3
soft palate 52
sound 49–51
   see also phonation; voice
speech behaviour, partner-oriented
   115
speech sounds, formation of 52–3
spinal column 76, 86, 88
spontaneous language 137–8, 142,
   159
stimulants, exercises as substitute
   for 72, 74
stories, telling 159
stress, and bodily tension 21
sulcus glottidis 178
support 18, 42–3, 48, 116–19
syllables
   final 143–4
   with modulation 134
   in speaking pitch 133
symptoms, meaning of 8, 10,
   15–16, 19

tai chi 24
teeth 52
therapist
   as method 26
   as a person 25–6
   relationship with client 14, 18,
      25, 26–7, 174
   requirements for 18, 168–9, 179
   and transparency 27–8, 169
   see also clients
throat, relaxing 101–2
throaty voices 140
timbre 51
tonal colour 51
tone 44–51, 52
tongue 52
tonus (body tension) 6, 18, 20, 22,
   29, 36
   and aims of therapy 165
   exercises 64–119

and intention 55–6, 108, 111
letting-go 92, 94, 107
and posture 36, 56
regulating 23–4, 55, 65–74, 90,
   118
transactional analysis 27
transfer 28–30, 158–61
   aid and options 160–1
   and behavioural change 29–30
   client's choice 170
   exercises 158–60
   problem of 28–9

upper partials 50–1, 184

valve function 41
valve tension 110
visualisation 12, 22
vocal cords 44
   length and density of 47–8
vocal fold vibration 35, 41, 45–7,
   126, 152, 178
   amplitude of 48
   frequency 47–8
vocal folds 44–5
   closing of 45
   paralysis 178
   polyps and nodules 179, 187
vocal tract 3, 52
   resonance 49, 122
voice
   calling 149–50
   changing vocal behaviour 5–6, 9
   control of 4–6
   as 'deep carrier' of language 3
   formation of 49–51
   and illness 6
   increasing sound level 145–6
   as instrument 4–6
   and person 3–4
   personal sound potential 134,
      136
   physiology of 3, 18, 36–7, 165
   and self 4–7, 175
voice disorders 6–7, 48–9, 177–89
   amateur singers 185
   children 181–3
   as communication disturbance
      27
   diagnosing 12–13, 177–8
   as expression of disorder of
      whole person 191

functional 49
and functional voice training 18
and intonation 180
organic 177–81
and rest 49
and singing voice 183–9
voice therapy
and amateur singers 185
and body tension 56
and professional singers 187–9
and psychotherapy 6–7
see also Person-Oriented Voice
Therapy (PVT)

volume 48, 184
vowel spaces 129–30
vowels
formation of 50–1, 52, 152–3, 185
use of 141–2

whispering 49
Wirth, G. 5–6, 42, 183, 184

yawning 122, 139
yoga 24

zen meditation 24